From the kitchens of The Soul Vegetarian

Soul
Vegetarian
Cookbook
Volume 2

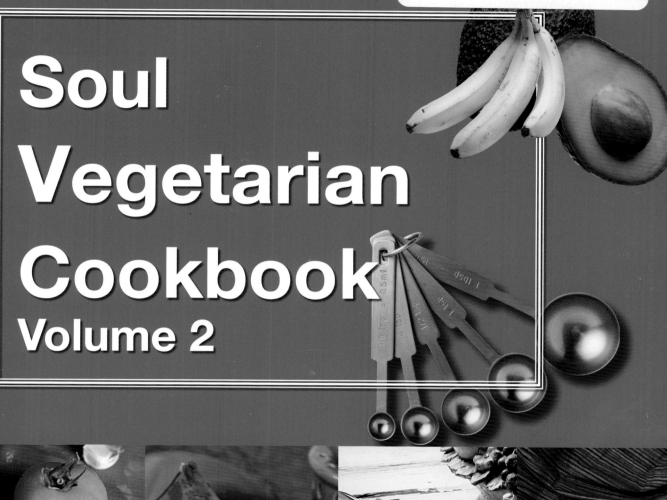

Published in cooperation with:
Divine Universal Sisterhood
Soul Vegetarian Restaurants
879 Ralph David Abernathy Blvd.
Atlanta, GA 30310

ISBN:0-942683-13-7
ISBN:978-0-942683-16-5 (2nd Printing)

The scriptural references used in this book are taken
from the New Scofield Reference Bible

DEDICATION

We extent a special tribute to Sister Karliyah Baht Israel, nutritionist, devoted and dedicated pioneer, mother, sister and teacher who contributed greatly to the creation and perfection of vegetarian nutrition. She determined that the path to improved physical well being is due in large proportion to diet transformation. Thus, as head nutritionist, Sister Karliyah guided this successful journey to vitality and longevity within our community through the application of healthier diet principles. This cookbook and nutritional guide represents our wish to share the successes pioneered by Sister Karliyah and others.

The Soul Vegetarian Cookbook is dedicated to all those brothers and sisters who labored untiringly throughout the years to make this information available for those seeking a new way of life through diet.

We recommend that you use high quality, whole food products to ensure that your recipes meet the high standards and optimum taste we have set for each dish.

The Soul Vegetarian Cookbook is your doorway to excellent health, good eating and longevity. We draw on the over forty –years of experience garnered in our quest for the optimum vegan diet to offer you premium nutrition, exciting taste and, a global variety of whole foods. Your wealth lies in your health.

These recipes are a creative and healthful awakening for all!!!

Bon Appetite!

B'tayah-vone!

To Your Health

Awards

Soul Vegetarian Restaurants have been the vanguard for healthy, nutritious, and savory food for over three decades. An unwavering commitment to eradicate sickness and disease through nutrition, means more than that. Soul Vegetarian Restaurants brand remains the most internationally recognized name for delicious, healthy comfort foods, and there are people behind that brand who genuinely work to ensure your well-being. We recognize the essential relationship between the human body, spirit, and the food that nourishes both. Thus, we seek to create an oasis wherein one can experience this consciousness for the fullest. Our objective is that Soul Vegetarian Restaurants are known eternally as the quintessential institution for healthy lifestyle.

1984 – Chicago Sun Times: One Restaurant Even Non-Vegetarians Can Appreciate

1986 – Critics Choice: Health Food That is Remarkably Good

1987 – Citizens Newspaper: Everything You Ever Dreamed Of in Soul Food

1987 – Washington Post: A Bit Better Than One Standard

1987 – Vegetarian Times: "It's Vegetarian Fare is Among The Best in The City"

1989 – Atlanta Magazine: Best Onion rings

1990 – Atlanta Magazine: Best Vegetarian Cuisine

1991 – Atlanta Magazine: Best Vegetarian Restaurant

1992 – Atlanta Magazine: Best of Atlanta. "Best Health Food"

1993 – Atlanta Magazine: Best of Atlanta: "Best Health Food"

1993 – Vegetarian Times: Down Home African American Cooking

1994 – The Washington Post: Offering Healthier Versions of Pizza and Burgers

1994 – The Washington Informer: Washington's "Finest" African American Restaurant

1996 – Vegetarian Times: Essential "Soulfulness" That Helps Define the African American Experience

1996 – Cleveland Plain Dealer: Vegan Cuisine with A "Soul Food Flair"

1996 – Cleveland Free Times Magazine: True Vegans

1997 – PETA Awards: People For Ethical Treatment of Animals (Catering)

1999 – ZAGAT Award: Food and Service

2000 – Vegetarian Times: 31 Top Vegetarian Restaurants; Soul Vegetarian, Atlanta, GA and Soul Vegetarian Exodus Café Washington, D.C.

2002 – PETA: Restaurant of the Month, Soul Vegetarian-Charleston, SC

2004 – Capitol City Bank & National African American Culinary Arts and Hospitality Association: Top One Hundred in America, Soul Vegetarian Restaurant South

2005 – AOL City Guide, Chicago: City's Best Healthy Dining Restaurant, Soul Vegetarian Restaurant

ACKNOWLEDGEMENTS

This cookbook is dedicated to the valiant pioneers
who paved the way and instituted the principles of nutrition,
health and longevity. We give a special acknowledgement to our
Emah (mother) Karliyah Baht Israel for
"The Sacred Diet" Divine Nutritional Guidelines
for the New Millennium.

I want to give special thanks
to all those who assisted with this extraordinary project,
and whose dedication helped make this all possible:
Prince Rahm and his family, Prince Immanuel and his family;
and to my Crowned Sisters,
whose incredible ability to stay focused on the vision aided
and nourished my spirit.

I extend a special thanks and appreciation to Brother
Ron Sanders for all of your meticulous work with the layout
design and photography.

I offer my gratitude to The Divine Jerusalem Sisterhood, who,
over a forty-year period, developed the recipes that formed the
basis of this sacred diet. You have performed a job will done.

The family of Soul Vegetarian Restaurant would like to thank all
of our customers, friends, and acquaintances for your many
years of continuous love, patronage, and contributions that
you have shared with us.

We are externally grateful and appreciative of your support.

TABLE OF CONTENTS

FOOD SECTIONS

INTRODUCTION

Dear Family,

Welcome to a new phase in the Soul Vegetarian experience. It has been more than 30 years since the opening of our first restaurant in Atlanta, Georgia. A few years thereafter, we published our first cookbook. We have grown in that time, learning how to enhance and raise the standards of what we offer you. All our recipes have been improved, reflecting our understanding of the deteriorating state of dietary health and our studied application of techniques and products that raise the quality of the vegan diet. For example, we promote the use of less and better quality oils, more natural sweeteners and less dependence on processed food products.

Our recipes have been re-examined, testing each to meet the highest standards of quality, taste, nutrition and presentation. We have done this for you, our family, our friends, our customers in our prayer that your health will be significantly improved while doing so you will enjoy the new, improved and delicious recipes in – SOUL VEGETARIAN COOKBOOK Volume 2.

This is our chance to provide delicious, nutritious meals for you and to share the wealth of the earth. Despite the increased information available about the significance of diet to our health, many people are confused about the right choices, in some cases give up trying to discern. We have come to understand that a holistic, regenerative diet based upon the same organic elements which comprise the human body are found in the earth from which man was created is the best diet for human consumption and health. You can rest assured that this is what we practice and advocate in our service to you.

And still, it occurred to me that a great many people do not consider that what we consume has a direct and lasting effect on the quality of our lives. This fear was verified by a recent study which revealed that only 14% of African American males consciously connected what they were eating to the state of their health. *(The National Cancer Institutes, "5 A Day For Better Health Program). This kind of information is invaluable. Therefore, we have taken time to include information about the preventable, diet-related diseases that are destroying people by the thousands.

Over the past two decades, we have come to understand that we can reduce and in some cases eradicate the effects of many of the top ten diet-related diseases such as cancer, hypertension, arteriosclerosis, diabetes and strokes just by adopting the proper diet. Studies have shown that diet and lifestyle choices including proper exercise, the right amount of water and sunshine, can in fact make a great difference in our health. It has been my privilege over the years to advise our clients and family that with the proper eating and drinking habits, we can experience a vibrant, more energetic life. However, the improper use of food and drink will in fact disrupt the natural cycles of the body – causing illness, disease, and eventually death.

I am brokenhearted when I look at current health statistics, in particularly cancer cases. Within the United States alone, it is estimated that more than 8 million cancer cases have been diagnosed. There were at least 150,000 new colon rectal cancer cases this year alone. Medical research has definitely established a probable link between colon rectal cancer and meat eating. It has long been established that the body's digestive system is not equipped to break down the fibers that meat contains. We really must face the fact that we are what we eat. If we continue to eat dead, dying and decaying animals -- then we cannot expect to have long and healthy lives.

We know that there is profit for some in our food addictions. Many of us swear by our taste to an addictive diet that has become for us too good to resist. Illness and death are a high price to pay as we lose our health. We work diligently to create vegan dishes with tastes and textures you have come to love to help you on your way to optimum health.

Remember, the recipes in the Soul Vegetarian Cookbook are all natural, non-dairy, free of any animal products, chemicals and without the deadly "whites" – sugar, flour, rice. The recipes do contain love in abundance! You are in for a treat and your taste buds will be more than satisfied. Because you show such love for your body, your body will love you back in excellent health and longevity.

Your senses of taste, smell, touch, sight, and feel will be enhanced and revived. You will have to reach back to your ancient collective memory to pull forward these dishes composed of the same fruits, vegetables, nuts, grains, seeds, legumes and complimentary whole food ingredients to relearn what is good for you.

Through it all, know that this is our humble contribution to the betterment of humanity and our service to the Creator, Yah. It is our prayer that it is found acceptable and inspirational.

Here's to good eating!

Yafah

"And God said, behold I have given you every bearing seed, which is upon the face of the earth, and every tree, in which is the fruit of a tree yielding seed; to you it shall be for food."

Genesis 1:29

WHAT IS A NUTRITION ROOM?

A nutrition room is much more than a traditional kitchen, it is the part of the home set aside for the planning and preparation of nutritional foods that will sustain and maintain the good health of the family.

With this definition in mind, we invite you to step through the door of our nutrition room. From here, you will embark on a journey that will lay before you a totally new experience within the realm of vegetarian cuisine.

For the past 32 years, we have concentrated on developing the skills and perfecting the methods which make the vegetarian diet nutritious, attractive and delicious. We believe we have achieved those goals. However, the final determination is up to you. These recipes are road maps to eternal life. Please follow them carefully and enjoy the journey.

Helpful Cooking Hints

1. A good cook must have these three important qualities:
    a. willing spirit   b. consistency   c. cleanliness

2. Use unprocessed whole grains· They are more nutritious·

3. Food which are three days old or older should not be used because either it has spoiled or has acquired a refrigerator taste· This procedure helps you to avoid un-healthy incidents·

4. Make lunch your heaviest meal· Eating heavy in the morning after the body has fasted or at a late hour can cause weight gain and stomach discomforts·

5. Avoid peeling vegetables unless absolutely necessary because many nutrients are found in the peelings·

6. You will use less spices when cooking at a medium-to-low flame because at that tem-perature, the spices cook through the food·

7. Recipes utilizing pickle relish should use the liquid from the relish to enhance the flavor·

8. When adding sea salt or other high sodium products, add a little at a time to the recipe, tasting after each measurement to ensure that dishes are not too salty·

9. Use seasonal food items as a practice to reap full nutritional benefits· Use organic or locally-grown fresh fruits and vegetables·

10. In recipes that call for margarine, use non-hydrogenated soy margarine. The brand we use "Earth Balance" is 100% vegan and is a natural butter spread.

11. All fruits and vegetables must be washed and rinsed with an all natural veggie wash.

12. Even though these recipes are perfectly measured, experienced cooks can add ingredients according to taste.

13. Serve brown rice with chickpeas or soybeans. It gives you a complete protein meal.

14. Always soak your beans, nuts, seeds, and grains for 24 hours before using them. This releases harmful digestive enzyme inhibitors. Cover these items with at least 3 inches of water. Drain and rinse them thoroughly after soaking.

15. Pasta cooked al dente is done but firm.

16. Read the labels on all food packages. Be aware of artificial colorings, preservatives, additives, and other harmful ingredients. Use organic packaged foods if needed.

HANDY RECIPE MEASUREMENT CONVERSION TABLE

KITCHEN MATH WITH METRIC TABLE

MEASURE	EQUIVALENT	METRIC ML)
1 Tbsp.	3 Tsp.	14.8 milliliters
2 Tbsp.	1 oz.	29.6 milliliters
1 jigger	1 ½ oz.	44.4 milliliters
¼ cup	4 Tbsp.	59.2 milliliters
⅓ cup	5 Tbsp. plus 1 tsp.	78.9 milliliters
½ cup	8 Tbsp.	118.4 milliliters
1 cup	16 Tbsp.	236.8 milliliters
1 pint	2 cups	473.6 milliliters
1 quart	4 cups	947.2 milliliters
1 liter	4 cups plus 3 ½ Tbsp.	1,000.0 milliliters
1 oz. (dry)	2 Tbsp.	28.35 grams
1 pound	16 oz.	453.59 grams
2.21 pounds	35.3 oz.	1.00 kilogram

THE APPROXIMATE CONVERSION FACTORS FOR UNITS OF VOLUME

TO CONVERT FROM	TO	MULTIPLY BY
teaspoons (tsp.)	milliliters (ml)	5
tablespoons (tbsp.)	milliliters (ml)	15
fluid ounces (fl. oz.)	milliliters (ml)	30
cups (c)	liters (1)	0.24
pints (pt.)	liters (1)	0.47
quarts (qt.)	liters (1)	0.95
gallons (gal.)	liters (1)	3.8
milliliters (ml)	fluid ounces (fl. oz.)	0.03
liters (1)	pints (pt.)	2.1
liters (1)	quarts (qts.)	1.06
liters (1)	gallons (gal.)	0.26

SIMPLIFIED MEASURES

dash = less than ⅛ teaspoon

3 tsp = 1 Tbsp·

16 Tbsp = 1 cup

1 cup = ½ pt·

2 cups = 1 pt·

2 pt· (4 c·) = 1 qt·

4 qt· (liquid) = 1 gal·

8 qt· (solid) = 1 peck

4 pecks = 1 bushel

16 oz· = 1 lb·

If you want to measure part-cups by the tablespoon· remember:

4 Tbsp· = ¼ cup

5 ⅓ Tbsp· = ⅓ cup

8 Tbsp· = ½ cup

10 ⅔ Tbsp = ⅔ cup

12 Tbsp· = ¾ cup

14 Tbsp· = ⅞ cup

Breads

Corn Bread

Corn Bread Patties

Flax Crackers

Hebrew Toast

Homemade Biscuits

No Bake Banana Bread

Pancakes

Whole-Wheat Cheese Toast

Whole Wheat Flour Batter

Zucchini Bread

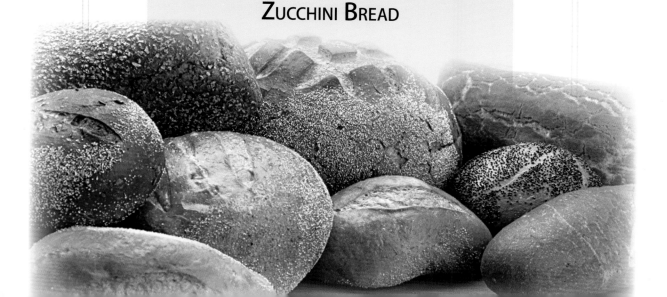

CORNBREAD

2 cups yellow corn meal
¼ cup soy flour
¼ cup wheat germ
¼ cup unbleached flour
½ tsp. aluminum free
   baking powder

4 tbsp. non-hydrogenated soy margarine
½ cup vegetable oil
¼ cup turbinado sugar
1 tsp. sea salt
4 cups filtered warm water

1. Mix all dry ingredients together, with whisk.

2. Melt oil and margarine together.

3. Add to dry mixture. Add water slowly until the right consistency is obtained. Mix well.

4. Bake 50 minutes at 325 degrees.

Yields: 4 servings

CORNBREAD PATTIES

1 cup corn meal
¼ stick non-hydrogenated soy margarine
2 tbsp. vegetable oil
1½ cups hot water

¼ cup whole wheat flour
⅛ tsp. vegetable sal
1 tbsp. turbinado sugar
2 tbsp. wheat germ

1. Mix dry ingredients well.

2. Add water, forming a batter of stiff consistency. Stir in sugar and margarine.

3. Heat oil in pan until hot. Pour oil into batter and stir.

4. Drop batter by the tablespoonsful into a lightly oiled skillet. (Three to four will fit in a medium skillet.)

5. Let cook until patties dry out on top side.

6. Turn over and let brown. Serve immediately.

Yields: 4 servings

FLAX CRACKERS

4 cups whole flax seeds,
  soaked 4 to 6 hours
⅓ cup liquid aminos
juice of 2 lemons

1. Soak flax seeds for 4 to 6 hours in purified water. You will then have a gelatinous mixture, be sure to keep moist and loose for spreading.

2. Add braggs and lemon juice and mix well.

3. Spread mixture as thin as possible on your dehydrator trays with a teflex sheet on top.

4. Dehydrate at 105 degrees for 5 to 6 hours and then flip the mixture and remove the teflex sheet.

6. Continue dehydrating until the mixture is completely dry. Approximately 5 to 6 hours.

Optional: You could add garlic, onions, taco seasoning, Italian seasoning, chili powder, cumin in any combination. Be creative and make up your own recipe.

Yields: 4 servings

HEBREW TOAST

1 cup soy milk
¼ cup turbinado sugar
1½ tsp. nutmeg
1½ tsp. cinnamon
1 tbsp. vanilla

1½ tsp. nutritional yeast
1 tbsp. oil
pinch sea salt
4 slices whole wheat bread

1. Blend all ingredients together.

2. Dip bread into mixture.

3. Grill on both sides in cast iron skillet.

Yields: 2 servings

HOMEMADE BISCUITS

2¼ cups unbleached flour
4   tbsp. non-hydrogenated soy
    margarine
½   tsp. sea salt
1   tbsp. aluminum free baking powder
1   cup soy milk
2   tbsp. turbinado sugar (optional)

1. In a medium bowl, mix dry ingredients.

2. Mix non-hydrogenated soy margarine,
   into 2 cups flour with a fork until flour becomes crumbly

3. Stir in milk just enough to wet the flour. Knead in the remaining flour.
   Roll dough on floured surface until 1½ inch thick.

4. Place on greased cookie sheet. Place in hot oven at 350 degrees for 15 minutes.

   Yields: 10 biscuits

PANCAKES

2 cups flour (unbleached or wheat)
4 tbsp. Aluminum free baking powder
½ tsp. sea salt
½ cup turbinado sugar (optional)
2 tsp. cinnamon
¼ tsp. nutmeg (optional)
4 tbps. filtered water

2 tbsp melted non-hydrogenated
   soy margarine
1 tsp. vanilla (optional)
1 cup plain soy milk
½ tsp. black strap molasses

1. Mix dry ingredients together.

2. Add remaining ingredients,
   mixing only until wet.

3. Use 4 oz ladle and drop onto
   a hot grill or pan.

Yields: 12 pancakes

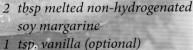

NO BAKE BANANA BREAD

2 cups brazil nuts
4 bananas
6 pitted medjool dates,
   soaked in water for 2 hours

2 tsp. cinnamon
1 cup walnuts

1. Place brazil nuts in food processor and process until mixture resembles flour.

2. Add 2 bananas, dates, and cinnamon to the processor and process until mixture is smooth.

3. Pour into a bowl and add 2 bananas cut into small pieces and chopped walnuts, stirring well.

4 Spoon mixture onto teflex sheets and spread to ½ inch thickness. Dehydrate for 4 hours.

5. Turn bread over and dehydrate on mesh sheet for an additional 4 hours until bread is almost dry.

6. Cut into pieces and dehydrate another hour.

Yields: 4 servings

WHOLE-WHEAT CHEESE TOAST

2 slices whole wheat bread
1 tbsp. soy cheese*
1 pat non-hydrogenated soy margarine (or 1 tbsp. unrefined oil)

* follow recipe on page 13

1. Spread soy cheese on whole wheat bread.
2. Brown in skillet with margarine.

WHOLE WHEAT FLOUR BATTER (WET AND DRY)

Instead of deep-frying our foods we use less oils with the batters. Normally we suggest using the dry batter but for extra coating and flavor, both wet and dry are used. Suggested foods: mushrooms, cauliflower, protein gluten, eggplant slices.

DRY BATTER

1 cup whole wheat flour
1 tbsp. garlic powder
¼ cup nutritional yeast

½ tsp. paprika
½ tbsp. vege sal

1. Sift flour and add all other dry ingredients. Mix well.
2. Cover foods completely with batter and place in skillet with desired oil (hot). Cook until done on all sides

WET BATTER

1 cup whole wheat flour
½ tsp. paprika
½ tsp. salt

1½ cups water
1 tsp. garlic powder
¼ cup tamari

1. Mix dry ingredients well and add water. Use more water or less for desired consistency.

2. When using the wet and dry batters together, begin with the wet batter. Completely immerse food pieces into wet batter and then completely cover wet pieces with the dry batter.

3. Place food pieces in skillet and cook as in dry batter recipe.

ZUCCHINI BREAD

3 cups whole wheat flour
2 tsp. cinnamon
1 tsp. nutmeg
1 tsp. allspice
1 tsp. sea salt

1 tsp. non aluminum baking soda
2 cups turbinado sugar
3 cups shredded zucchini
1 cup unrefined oil
1 tsp. vanilla

1. Sift dry ingredient together. In a separate bowl, mix oil and sugar.

2. Add vanilla and zucchini.

3. Add dry mixture and mix well. Bake in loaf pans 350 degree for 35 minutes or until done.

Yield: 4 servings

Sauces and Gravies

Avocado Salsa
Barbecue Sauce
Brown Vegetable gravy
Green Pea Mushroom Sauce
Hot Sauce
Marinade Sauce
Nutritional Yeast Gravy
Soy A Nase
Soy Cheese Sauce
Sweet And Sour Sauce
Tahini Sauce
Tomato Sauce With Basil
Tartar Sauce

Avocado Salsa

2 ripe avocados, diced
1 small red bell pepper, diced
1 small green bell pepper, diced
1 medium carrot, peeled and sliced
1 medium tomato, diced
½ small red onion, diced

½ tsp. sea salt
¾ cup pitted olives
¼ cup fresh lime juice
1 tsp. cayenne pepper
3 tbsp. minced cilantro

1. Process bell peppers, carrot, tomato and onion to a fine chop in the food processor or finely chop vegetables by hand.

2. Add remaining ingredients except avocado. Mix well.

3. Fold in diced avocado and serve.

Yields: 4 servings

Bar-B-Que Sauce

5   tbsp. turbinado sugar or other sweetener
1½ tsp. apple cider vinegar
1   cup filtered water
2   tbsp. vegetable oil

12 oz. can tomato paste
3   tbsp. blackstrap molasses
2   tbsp. garlic powder
¼   tsp. sea salt

1. Place all ingredients in large sauce pan.

2. Simmer over low heat for 20 minutes. Stir occasionally.

Use over protein glutens, spaghetti or your favorite main dish.

Yields: 2 cups

BROWN VEGETABLE GRAVY

10 button mushrooms (sliced)
1 cup whole wheat flour
1 stalk celery (diced)
2 tbsp. unrefined oil
4 tbsp. tamari

1. Sauté flour and oil in a medium size pot.

2. Stir with wire whisk and allow gravy to brown.

3. Pour water while stirring with whisk.

4. Add remaining ingredients and simmer for 15 minutes.

Yields: 4 servings

FRESH TOMATO SAUCE WITH BASIL

5 medium tomatoes (chopped)
4 tsp. garlic minced
6 tsp. extra virgin olive oil
1 tbsp. lemon or lime juice

½ cup fresh basil chopped
½ tsp. spike
cayenne to taste

1. Sauté garlic in olive oil over medium heat for about 1 minute or until it begins to brown.

2. Quickly add tomatoes cover and simmer for 10 minutes.

3. Add remaining ingredients to pan, cover and simmer for 3 minutes longer.
Season to taste.

4. May be layered over noodles or added to a stir fry.

5. Serve hot.

Yields: 4 servings

GREEN PEA MUSHROOM SAUCE

1 lb. dried green peas (soaked overnight)
2 lbs. mushrooms (sliced)
2 tbsp. non-hydrogenated soy margarine (optional)
1 tsp. sea salt

1. Rinse peas and boil until soft

2. Blend peas and 1/2 of the mushrooms
   in blender until creamy and return to heat.

3. Add remaining mushrooms, soy margarine and salt.

Yields: 2 cups

HOT SAUCE

2 tsp. olive oil
1 tsp. basil
1 level tsp. sea salt
5 oz. filtered water

6 oz. can organic tomato paste
2 tbsp. turbinado sugar or other sweetener
3 tbsp. apple cider vinegar
¾ cup grated and pressed garlic
½ tsp. cayenne pepper

1. Mix all ingredients well.

2. Add water to desired consistency.

Yields: 1½ cups

LIVE MARINADE

2 cloves garlic minced
½ cup onions

1 cup virgin olive oil
4 tbs. lemon juice
1 tsp sea salt (optional)

Combine all ingredients in a bowl and mix well.

Use this marinade sauce to marinate tofu, red and green pepper,
mushrooms, or onions.

Yields: 1 cup

NUTRITIONAL YEAST GRAVY

2½ cups filtered water
2   tbsp. vegetable oil
1   tsp. granulated garlic powder
½   cup diced onions
½   cup diced red peppers

¼   cup whole wheat flour
½   cup nutritional yeast
⅛   tsp. paprika
⅛   tsp. curry powder
⅓   cup liquid aminos

1. Sauté vegetables in oil.   Add flour and nutritional yeast and with a wire whisk, stir well.

2. Allow flour to brown then add water. Continue to whisk and add seasonings.

3. Simmer on low flame. Add mushrooms if desired.

Yields: 2 cups

SOY A NASE (SOY BUTTER)

1   cup soy milk
½   cup silken tofu
½   cup vegetable oil

1. Place milk in blender. Start blending on medium speed. As milk blends, a hole will form in the center.

2. Add the silken tofu and pour oil slowly into the hole until it closes. The hole in the center should be completely closed.

3. Stir well, mixture should be stiff.

Use in cream pies, on sandwiches and when recipes call for soy butter.

Yields: 2 cups

SOY CHEESE SAUCE

2 cups soy butter (follow recipe above)
4 tbsp. nutritional yeast
½ tsp. paprika
⅛ tsp. garlic powder
⅛ cup tamari

1. Blend all ingredients together until creamy and has a smooth texture as cheese.

2. Chill until ready to use.

3. Use in any recipes that call for soy cheeses.

Yields: 2 cups

SWEET AND SOUR SAUCE

3 cups pineapple juice
1 cup turbinado sugar or other sweetener
1 tbsp. powdered ginger

4 tbsp. arrowroot powder
½ cup filtered water
½ cup tamari

1. Simmer all ingredients except ½ of the water in a sauce pan over medium heat for 5 minutes.

2. Add remaining water to cornstarch to form a paste, stirring constantly.

3. Cook until thickened to desired consistency.

Serve over spring rolls, shish kabobs, browned spicy protein gluten slices or sweet and sour vegetables.
Yields: 3 cups

TAHINI SAUCE

1   cup tahini
½   cup lemon juice
¼   cup olive oil
1   tsp. sea salt
1½ cups filtered water

Yields: 1½ servings

1. Blend all ingredients well.

2. Serve as a dipping sauce with chickpea patties, roasted eggplant sticks, toasted pita bread.

3. Can be used as a salad dressing.

TARTAR SAUCE

1½ cups soy butter (see page 13)
⅛ tsp. mustard

1   cup pickle relish
1½ tbsp. maple syrup
1   tsp. sea salt

1. Blend all ingredients except relish

2. Remove from blender and add relish.

Yields: 2½ cups

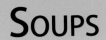

Soups

Broccoli Soup

Brown Lentil Soup

Ground Nut Soup

Low Sodium Celery Soup

Potato Soup

Orange Lentil Soup

Chili Olé

Vegetable Soup

Vegetable Noodle Soup

Broccoli Soup

8 cups chopped broccoli flowerets
4 med. potatoes (diced small)
4 stalks celery (diced)
3 tbsp. nutritional yeast (optional)
1 tbsp. garlic powder

1 tbsp. sea salt
1 tbsp. onion powder
1 gallon filtered water
½ tsp. basil

1. Cook potatoes with ½ tsp. sea salt until soft.

2. Bring to a boil.

3. Add remaining ingredients then lower heat.

4. Simmer for 40 minutes.

Yields: 8 servings

Brown Lentil Soup

3 cups brown lentil beans
12 cups filtered water
¼ tbsp. dried minced onions
½ cup chopped onion
½ cup diced celery
2 tbsp. non hydrogenated
   soy margarine, or unrefined
   oil (optional)

2 cloves garlic
1 tbsp. granulated garlic
1 tbsp. sea salt
2 tsp. basil
1 tsp. curry powder
1 tsp. paprika powder

1. Soak lentil beans overnight.

2. Cook lentil beans and vegetables in water until tender.

3. Add remaining ingredients. Simmer 15 minutes.

Yields: 8 Servings

GROUND NUT SOUP

1 15 oz jar natural unsweetened
   smooth peanut butter or almond
   butter
10 cups filtered water
2 cups zucchini squash (diced)
2 cups eggplant (diced)
2 cups onions (diced)
1 cup okra (sliced)
½ cup mushrooms (sliced)

½ cup tomato paste
½ tsp. hot sesame oil
1 tsp. sea salt
2 tsp. curry powder
2 tbsp. granulated garlic
1 tbsp. onion powder
2 tbsp. tamari

1. Mix peanut butter with enough water to dissolve the peanut butter to a smooth or loose consistency.

2. Put mixture into a large pot and let the peanut butter cook on low heat for thirty (30) minutes or until you see the oil separating from the peanut butter. (Make sure that you watch this carefully and not allow the peanut butter to stick to the bottom of the pot.)

3. Add the remainder of water and allow the peanut butter and water to come to a boil.

4. Add the tomato paste to the mixture and cook on medium heat for 10 minutes.

5. Add all the vegetables and stir.

6. Let the soup cook until the vegetables get tender; then add all the seasonings.

Simmer for 10-15 minutes. Soup will thicken as it cools.

Yields: 10 servings

LOW SODIUM CELERY SOUP

3 cups celery (chopped)
4 cups soy milk
¾ cup onions (diced)
3 tbsp. whole wheat flour
2 cups filtered water

1 tbsp. non hydrogenated soy margarine
2 tbsp. parsley
1 tsp. spike seasoning
¼ tsp. sea salt

1. In a medium pot, combine celery, onions and water. Cook for 12-15 minutes or until tender.

2. In a large skillet, melt margarine, blend in flour and add seasonings. Stir until thick. Add milk and simmer, stirring occasionally.

3. Add this sauce to the pot, and cook for 15 minutes longer. Stir occasionally until soup thickens.

4. Garnish with parsley.

Yields: 4 servings

POTATO SOUP

4 medium size potatoes
2 cloves garlic
1 tbsp. vege sal
½ tbsp. basil

½ cup soy milk or other milk such as
   almond, hemp, or rice milk
¼ cup nutritional yeast
5 quarts filtered water

1. Wash and dice potatoes.

2. Cook in a medium size pot until almost done.

3. Add all other ingredients. Simmer until done.

Yields: 4 Servings

ORANGE LENTIL SOUP

6 cups filtered water
2 cups orange lentil beans
5 celery stalks (diced)
1 medium onion (diced)
1 large carrot (diced)

1 potato (diced)
1 tbsp. garlic powder
2 tbsp. non-hydrogenated soy margarine
2 tsp. sea salt

1. Bring orange lentils up to a boil, then turn heat down very low.

2. Skim off white foam from top.

3. Cook orange lentils for 20 minutes with vegetables. Add remain
   ing ingredients and cook for 40 minutes stirring occasionally with
   a whisk.

4. Simmer until done.

Yields: 8 servings

CHILI OLÉ

8 cups filtered water
3 cloves garlic (diced)
1 lb. red beans
1 tbsp. chili powder
1 cup mushrooms
2 tbsp. molasses
2 stalks celery

2 tbsp. brown sugar
1 tbsp. cumin
½ cup onions
¼ red pepper
½ cup tomato paste
½ cup tamari

1. Cook beans, add molasses, cumin, turbinado sugar, chili
   powder, and tomato paste until done.

2. Sauté celery, onions and peppers.

3. Add sautéed vegetables to chili.

4. Simmer on medium heat for 10 minutes.

5. Add fresh garlic and mushrooms while
   chili is simmering.

Yields: 4 servings

VEGETABLE SOUP

1 cup broccoli, diced
1 cup potatoes, diced
1 cup carrots, diced
1 cup celery, diced
½ cup fresh corn
½ cup fresh string beans

1 tbsp. vege sal
1 tsp. oregano
1 tsp. basil
3 cloves of garlic
2 cups tomato paste
1 gallon water

1. Bring water to boil.   Add potatoes, string beans, and carrots, and return to boil.

2. Cook for 10 minutes. Add remaining ingredients.

3. Simmer on medium heat for 10 minutes. Stir in tomato paste and remove from heat.

Yields: 4 servings

VEGETABLE NOODLE SOUP

3 tbsp. non-hydrogenated soy margarine
2 tbsp. garlic powder
2 tbsp. nutritional yeast
1 tsp. paprika
1 tbsp. sea salt
6 oz. tomato paste
12 cups filtered water

4 oz. pkg noodles
3 med. tomatoes (sliced)
3 ears corn
2 med. onions (sliced)
2 stalks celery (diced)
1 small eggplants (diced)
1 med. red bell pepper (diced)
1 stalk broccoli
½ head cauliflower (sliced)

1. In a large cast iron skillet, saute tomatoes, eggplant, onions, peppers and non-hydrogenated soy margarine.

2. In a medium pot, mix sauteed vegetables, water, tomato paste, garlic powder and paprika.

3. When soup comes to a boil, add noodles, salt and nutritional yeast, turn down heat and cook until noodles are al dente.

4. Add broccoli at the end when soup is done.

Yields: 4 servings

Main Dishes
Protein (Gluten)

Southern Negev Bar-B-Que Twists

Protein Roast

Garvey Burgers

Garvey Loaf

Nubian Nuggets

Raw Gluten

RAW GLUTEN

1 quart water   *2 lbs. whole wheat flour*

1. Mix whole wheat flour with water into a firm texture. Make sure all flour is mixed well (medium to firm dough).

2. Let set for 45 minutes (no less).

3. Put dough in a colander. Run cold water while squeezing the dough to wash out starch from mixture.

4. Keep rinsing until all graininess is removed and water is clear from rinsing.

5. Cover with water until ready to use.

Yields: 1 lb.

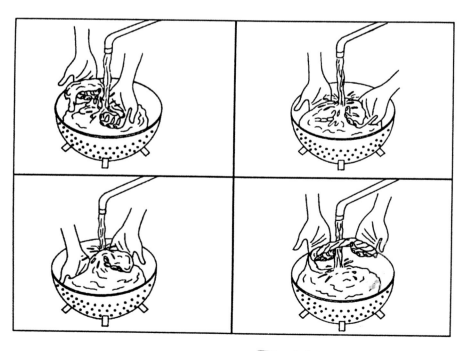

SOUTHERN NEGEV BAR-B-QUE TWISTS

2 lbs. raw gluten	1 tbsp. paprika
1½ cup nutritional yeast	1 tbsp. garlic powder
½ cup of peanut butter	1 medium onion (chopped fine)
⅓ cup tamari	½ cup hot oil
	1 cup bar-b-que sauce

1. In a large bowl, add tamari, yeast, garlic powder and paprika to raw gluten. Mix well by pulling and stretching.

2. Sauté onions in oil. Add peanut butter and hot oil to seasoned gluten. (Hot oil breaks the gluten down and helps the seasonings to penetrate.)

3. Continue to mix gluten well by pulling and stretching until consistency is stringy but doesn't tear apart.

4. Pull off small pieces of gluten and stretch and twist pieces into shapes similar to 6-8 inch bread sticks.

5. Place twists on lightly oiled cookie sheet and bake at 350 degrees for ½ hour or until crispy and brown on bottom. Brush twists with bar-b-que sauce and bake 10 minutes longer.

Yields: 12 twists

GARVEY LOAF

2½ cups raw gluten, boiled then ground
    in food processor
¼ cup whole wheat flour
2 tbsp. paprika
1 small bell pepper (chopped fine)

1 cup dried onion
2 tbsp. garlic powder
¼ tbsp. tamari sauce, or salt substitute
¼ cup oil

1. Add all ingredients to ground gluten and mix well.

2. Shape into a loaf. Bake in loaf pan at 350 degrees for 1½ hours.

3. During last 15 minutes, cover loaf with one of our favorite sauces: fresh tomato basil sauce, BBQ sauce, vegetable gravy or nutritional yeast gravy.

    Yields: 10 servings

GARVEY BURGERS

1. Follow recipe for Garvey Loaf.

2. Shape into patties. Cook patties on both sides until browned in lightly oiled skillet, or in a pan in the oven at 300°F.

Yields: 10 servings

NUBIAN NUGGETS

1 lb. raw gluten
1 gallon filtered water
1 cup nutritional yeast
2 tbsp. sea salt

2 tbsp. garlic powder
2 tbsp. curry powder
⅛ cup bar-b-que sauce

1. Add all ingredients except gluten to water and bring to a boil.

2. Cut gluten into 4-6 inch pieces and drop into boiling water.

3. Stir occasionally until water comes to a second boil. Do not cover. Cook for 1 hour on medium heat.

4. Remove from heat and allow to cool.

5. Remove gluten from water and cut about 1/2 inch thick slices like steaks. Dry batter in seasoned flour or cornmeal and brown in lightly oiled skillet.

Serve with bar-b-que sauce.   Yields: 8 servings

PROTEIN ROAST

5 lbs. raw gluten
2 celery stalk (diced
2 tbsp. garlic powder
1 sweet pepper (diced)
2 tbsp. paprika
1 large onion (diced)
1 tbsp. sweet basil

2 carrots (diced)
2 tbsp. marjoram
4 cups water for basting
1 cup nutritional yeast
1 cup tamari
½ cup oil

1. Place raw gluten in a mixing bowl. Mix, pull and stretch gluten with seasonings. Add oil, tamari and yeast. Mix well.

2. Add vegetables and evenly distribute.

3. Form seasoned gluten into loaf and place in roasting pan. Add water to pan and cover.

4. Bake in roasting pan at 275 degrees for 45 minutes. Baste occasionally as it becomes brown.

5. Slice and serve.

SPECIAL TIPS: Serve with gravy or your favorite sauce.   Yields: 12 servings

Main Dishes
Grain

Amirah's Alabama-

(Spooned) Cornbread-Vegetable Dressing

Fluffy Millet

Hebrew Rice

Jollouf Rice (Ghana's Most Popular Dish)

Negev Bulgar (Cracked Wheat) Patties

AMIRAH'S ALABAMA (SPOONED)
CORNBREAD - VEGETABLE DRESSING

1 cup cornmeal
1 cup whole wheat flour
1½ tbsp. unrefined oil
½ cup vegetable oil
1¾ cups Filtered water
½ cup red peppers
½ cup green peppers
½ cup celery - (diced fine)
½ cup onion - (diced fine)

½ cup squash
½ cup string beans (diced fine)
1 tbsp. powdered sage
½ tsp. caynenne pepper
1 tsp. garlic Powder
1 tsp. poultry seasoning
3 tbsp. liquid aminos
1 cup bread crumbs
¼ tsp sea salt

1. Combine cornmeal and flour in mixing bowl. Heat oil with non-hydrogenated soy margarine in the oven in a baking pan.

2. Pour heated oil combination into cornmeal mix along with 1 cup of water. Mix well.

3. Pour into a baking dish. Bake 30 minutes at 300 degrees. Set aside to cool.

4. Saute vegetables in sauce pan with a little non-hydrogenated soy margarine or olive oil. Add seasonings and liquid aminos.

5. Crumble cornbread mixture, bread crumbs, vegetable mixture and re maining water. Mix well

6. Place dressing in baking dish and bake 30 minutes at 300 degrees.

Yields: 8 servings

FLUFFY MILLET

¾ cup filtered water   1 cup millet
¼ tsp. sea salt   1 tbsp. unrefined oil

1. Bring water to a boil and add salt.

2. Stir in millet with a whisk and boil for five minutes.

3. Turn down heat and simmer for 35 minutes.

4. Turn off heat. Let steam for 5 minutes.

5. Add oil (flax seed or olive oil) before serving.

Note: Millet is one of seven grass seeds that are high in iron and protein. It is nutritional as well as rich in calcium. Delicious topped with grilled tomatoes, onions, mushroom, or your favorite gravy. Makes a great base for meatless dishes.

Yields: 2 servings

HEBREW RICE

3 cups cooked brown rice
1 medium red and green bell
   pepper (chopped medium)
2 large cloves garlic (minced)
½ cup broccoli (chopped)
3 tbsp. tamari

1 cup fresh mushrooms (sliced thin)
2 tbsp. olive oil
2 medium onions (chopped medium)
¼ cup carrots (chopped)

1. Sautee vegetables in oil in a large skillet or saucepan.

2. Slowly add rice to vegetables and mix thoroughly.

3. Add garlic and tamari.

Yields: 4 servings

JOLLOUF RICE
(GHANA's'S MOST POPULAR DISH)

1½ lbs. fresh tomatoes (sliced thin)
1 cup shredded cabbage
1 cup fresh spring peas
2½ cups tomato paste
¼ cup tamari
I cup string beans (cut into bite-sized pieces)

5 oz. palm oil
2¼ lbs. brown rice
1 cup diced carrots
3 large onions
3 cups water
1 tsp. sea salt

1. Heat palm oil in skillet. Sauté onions until light brown.

2. Gradually stir in tomato paste and cook.

3. Add 1/4 cup water and 1 tsp. salt.

4. Stir in vegetables; allow to steam.

5. Add rice and remaining water and salt; stir twice while cooking.

6. Allow to steam, reduce heat and simmer until done.

Yields: 20 servings

NEGEV BULGAR
(CRACKED WHEAT) PATTIES

4 tbsp. whole wheat flour (level)
2 tbsp. paprika
⅓ cup oil
1½ tbsp. tamari

½ 1b. bulgar
3 tbsp. peppers (chopped fine)
3 tbsp. onions (chopped fine)
½ bulb garlic (chopped fine)
1½ tbsp. ground sage

1. Pre-cook bulgar in pot with just enough water to cover until all water is absorbed. Cool.

2. Add sage, chopped vegetables, paprika, tamari and flour to cooked bulgar. Mix well.
3. Shape into patties and saute in oil on both sides until browned.

Yields: 4 servings

Main Dishes
Pasta

Lasagna

Macaroni and Cheese

LASAGNA

1 package lasagna strips
2 tbsp. nutritional yeast
1 tbsp. garlic powder
  salt (to taste)
2 tbsp. vege sal
2 tbsp. basil
1 red pepper (sliced thin)
1 green pepper (sliced thin)
1 block tofu 8 oz.

1 medium onion (sliced thin)
1 tbsp. olive oil
1 tbsp. vegetable oil
1 tbsp. paprika
2 lbs. gluten (boiled & ground)
1 cup filtered water
1 cup tomato paste
1 cup soy cheese*

* follow recipe on page 13

1. Boil lasagna strips al denté. (See Helpful Hints section)

2. Sauté crumbled gluten in skillet with 1 tbsp. vegetable oil, 1 tbsp. vege sal, 1 tbsp. basil.

3. Make sauce by mixing 1 cup tomato paste, 1 cup filtered water, 1 tbsp. basil, 1 tbsp. oil, 1 tbsp. vege sal and nutritional yeast. Bring to boil and let simmer for 15 minutes.

4. Layout lasagna strips in baking pan. Spread cheese over gluten then spread tomato sauce, peppers and onions. Continue layer ing in this manner until all ingredients are used.

5. Top with remaining tomato sauce and bake for 20 minutes at 350 degrees.

Yields: 8 servings

MACARONI & CHEESE

8 oz. macaroni noodles
2 cups soy cheese*
½ tsp. sea salt
* follow recipe on page 13

7   cups filtered water
2 tbsp. non-hydrogenated
   soy margarine

1. Cook noodles al denté with sea salt. Drain in colander. Run cold water over noodles to stop cooking process.
2. Mix 1½ cups of soy cheese with noodles. Mix well.
3. Place in lightly oiled casserole dish. Top with pats of non-hydrogenated soy margarine.
4. Spread remaining ½ cup of soy cheese on top of noodles.
5. Bake at 350 degrees for 20 minutes. Allow to cool before slicing.

   Yields: 4 servings

Main Dishes
Vegetable

Beet Loaf

Blackeyed Peas

Down-Home Greens

Cauliflower-In-A-Basket

Cheesy Potatoes

Eggplant Parmesan

Kale Greens

Village Of Peace Pot Pie

Oven Browned Potatoes

Picnic Potato Salad

Stuffed Eggplant

BEET LOAF

1 large carrot
1 tbsp. celery (chopped fine)
1 tbsp. onions (chopped fine)
1 clove garlic (minced)
2 tbsp. whole wheat flour

1 tbsp. paprika
1 medium beet
1 tbsp. peppers (chopped fine)
⅓ cup cornmeal
½ tbsp. tamari sauce

1. Grate beet and carrot on fine side of grater. Mix thoroughly with other ingredients.

2. Shape into loaf and place into an oiled 9 inch pan. Bake at 350 degrees for 45 minutes. Loaf can be covered with sauce or gravy.

(Potatoes can be substituted for beets)

Yields: 5 servings

BLACKEYE PEA PATTIES

⅓ cup of each vegetable carrots, onions, broccoli, green & red peppers - chopped fine
4 cloves of garlic
½ tsp. vege sal
1 tsp. basil

1 tsp. parsley flakes
1 tsp. cumin
1 tsp. garlic powder
1 tsp. onion powder
2 tsp. liquid aminos
1½ cups whole wheat flour
¼ cup water

Soak 2 cups of black eyes peas overnight
(NOTE: Beans will swell twice their size.)

1. In a blender, blend 1 cup of soaked peas with ¼ cup of water along with garlic and ½ of onion. Do this until all the beans are blended.

2. Mix with remaining vegetables. Add seasonings and mix thoroughly.

3. Slowly add whole wheat flour until mixture will hold together and is still moist.

4. Shape into small patties and place in a heated, oiled cast iron skillet.

5. Cook patties 5-7 minutes on each side. Continue cooking on both sides until done.

Yields: 5 servings

DOWN-HOME GREENS

1 bunch collards (or other greens)
2 medium onions (cut in rings)
1 medium eggplant (chopped fine)

2 tbsp. garlic (chopped fine)
1 cup water
2 medium tomatoes (sliced)
½ cup oil
salt (to taste)

1. Shred greens.

2. Cook in large skillet or medium pot in ½ cup oil and 1 cup water or in pressure cooker with eggplant for 12 minutes.

3. Sauté onions with tomatoes. Add garlic and salt to taste. Stir into greens.

Yields: 4-6 servings

CAULIFLOWER-IN-A-BASKET

1 medium head cauliflower
1 lb. whole wheat flour
½ tbsp. paprika
¾ tbsp. garlic powder

1 tbsp. sea salt
⅓ cup oil
⅔ cup water
tamari sauce (to taste)

1. Clean and separate cauliflower into individual bite-sized pieces.

2. Sift flour and add garlic powder, paprika and salt. Mix well.

3. Take ⅓ of flour batter, mix with tamari sauce, water and ¾ tbsp. of oil and stir into a creamy paste.

4. Place pieces of cauliflower in wet batter, then into dry batter.

5. Brown in skillet on medium flame or in oven at 300°F.

6. Brown slowly on all sides until tender.

7. Other vegetables like mushrooms, carrots, broccoli, etc. can be battered in this manner.

Yields: 3-4 servings

CHEESY POTATOES

1 tsp. vege sal
1 tbsp. paprika

2 lbs. white potatoes (sliced)
1 cup soy cheese *
¼ cup parsley

follow recipe on page 13

1. Wash and steam potatoes al dente. Do not overcook.

2. In a large baking pan, alternate layers of sliced potatoes and soy cheese. Top with remaining layer of soy cheese.

3. Sprinkle paprika and parsley on top

4. Bake at 350 degrees for thirty minutes or until cheese is brown.

Yields: 4-5 servings

EGGPLANT PARMESAN

3 medium eggplants
4 cups soy cheese*
¼ cup lemon juice
   whole wheat batter, wet and dry
3 tbsp. corn meal
2 large onions (thinly
   sliced)
12 oz. can tomato paste
¼ cup oil
1 tbsp. blackstrap molasses
¼ tsp. brown sugar

follow recipe on page 13

1. Add cornmeal to dry batter.

2. Slice eggplant lengthwise into thin slices.

3. Dip eggplant slices into wet batter, then into dry batter.

4. Brown battered slices in skillet in 1/8 cup oil, or in lightly oiled oven pan at 350°F.

5. Make sauce using tomato paste, molasses, brown sugar and
   lemon juice.

6. In ungreased oven pan, layer sauce, battered eggplant slices, thinly sliced onions, soy
   cheese. Layer in this manner until all ingredients have been used, allowing cheese to be
   last layer.

7. Bake at 350 degrees for approximately 20 minutes or until parmesan is firm.

Yields: 8 servings

VILLAGE OF PEACE POT PIE

Step 1 - Filling

1 lb. potatoes (diced medium or fine)
3 carrots (diced medium or fine)
½ cup celery (diced medium or fine)
1 green pepper (diced medium or fine)
1 lb. onions (diced medium or fine)
1 8 oz. package dried vegetables
1 lb. string beans (optional)
½ cup oil
½ tsp. salt

Step 2 - Gravy

1 cup nutritional yeast gravy

Step 3 - Crust

2 lbs. whole wheat flour
2 sticks non-hydrogenated soy margarine or ¾ cup oil
¼ cup oil
½ cup water

1. Rub margarine and flour together until it reaches the texture of coarse cornmeal. Add in oil, and ½ cup water. Mix well until dough is formed.

2. Roll out dough, fit into shape of baking pan. Use rest of dough for top crust.

3. Steam potatoes and vegetables until almost done. Add remaining ingredients. Pour mixture into crust with gravy.

4. Add top crust. Prick crust with fork to vent steam.

5. Bake pie at 350 degrees until crust is browned on top and bottom.

Yields: 10-12 servings

STUFFED EGGPLANT

2 tbsp. fresh parsley (chopped fine)
2 small peppers (chopped fine)
2 small onions (chopped fine)
2 small celery stalks (chopped fine)
1 small tomato (diced fine)

2 tbsp. tamari sauce, or other
    salt substitute
1½ tbsp. garlic powder
¼ cup brown rice
1 tbsp. paprika
2 medium eggplants

1. Cut eggplant in half. Scoop out the inside of the eggplant with a spoon. Break up with a fork.

2. Pre-cook eggplant shells in 1 cup boiling water for 5 minutes.

3. Cook rice.

4. Mix eggplant, pepper, onion, celery, and tomato well. Add rice, paprika, garlic powder, tamari and parsley. Continue to mix well.

5. Stuff each eggplant shell with filling, place on a lightly oiled oven pan and bake at 350 degress for 1/2 hour.

Yields: 4 servings

OVEN BROWNED POTATOES

8 potatoes
3 tbsp. olive oil

2 tbsp. spike
2 tbsp. garlic powder

1. Cut potatoes into quarters. Place in a deep oven pan.

2. Sprinkle with seasonings and oil. Mix potatoes and seasonings together in oven pan.

3. Bake in oven 350 degrees for 30-45 minutes. Stir potatoes occsionally until potatoes are done when they are brown outside and soft inside.

Yields: 8 servings

PICNIC POTATO SALAD

7 medium potatoes
1 medium onion
1 small red pepper (diced finely)
1 small green pepper (diced finely)
⅔ cup stalks of celery (diced finely)

½ cup pickle relish
1 tbsp. sea salt
1½ cups soy butter
½ tbsp. mustard

1. Boil potatoes and cube.

2. Mix all ingredients well. Serve chilled.

Yields: 8 servings

44

KALE GREENS

2-3 small bunches of chopped kale 4 tbsp. olive oil
1   medium onion (chopped)   1 tsp. sea salt
4   cloves of fresh garlic (minced)

1. Pre-heat one (1) tbsp. olive oil in a large pot or cast iron skillet.

2. Add onion and fresh garlic to olive oil and sauté the veggies until clear. Add the rest of the seasonings and sauté for another minute. Add the greens.

3. Cover greens with the appropriate lid. Steam for about 20 minutes or until tender. Stir occasionally. Add the remaining olive oil after greens are done.

Kale is rich in antioxidants, which help fight cancer, high in vitamin A, and very high in calcium.

MAIN DISHES
TOFU DISHES

BAKED TOFU

BLACK SESAME TOFU STIR FRY

NEAT HEBREWS

SCRAMBLED TOFU

TOFULAFELS

THE JOY OF SOY - TOFU

The only common plant food that contains complete protein, soy--popular in China for at least 5,000 years-is also fortified with ninja-like isoflavones . These are phyto (plant) estrogens. Soy has been proven to reduce the risk of coronary heart disease. It's proven promising in promoting bone health. Over the years, various studies have linked soy to breast-cancer prevention both in animal studies and in large-scale epidemiological research, which has found lower

breast-cancer rates linked to soy consumption among Asian women. In 1990, a National Cancer Institute workshop identified no fewer than five potential anti-carcinogens in soybeans. Thanks to all the glowing health benefits attributed to the legume, which had racked up about 7,000 medical-research citations, soy is the basis for a wonderful product that can be turned into thousands and thousands of wonderful Tofu products.

Tofu is the soybean curd that is solidified from the soy milk. Tofu is sometimes known as soy cheese, and comes in blocks packaged in water. Tofu is very high in protein but low in fat, making it an ideal product for creating dishes that are tasty, nutritional and low in calories. This product is the major stable protein source in not only China but Japan as well.

Tofu has two broad categories - firm and soft Tofu.

The firm Tofu is quite versatile because of its density and firmness allowing for stir fry, baking, roasting, and even the occasional frying. Firm Tofu like all Tofu, absorbs the flavors of the spices and vegetables being used. Silken Tofu which has a creamy texture is best for soups and deserts and allows for the making of, if you can believe this, whipped cream - a great treat.

All kinds of Tofu - extra firm, soft and silken can be found in most major grocery stores as well as health food shops and emporiums. For best results Tofu must be refrigerated. When using, remember to pour the water off, rinse, and then have fun with the recipes that make this product so enjoyable.

Tofu itself does not have a taste which makes it a perfect product to be used in all of your favorite recipes and the ones we have to share with you. Once you have experienced the Soul Vegetarian Tofu you will wonder how you prepared foods all these years without it.

With its vast versatility, Tofu can be used firm and tossed in salads, stir fry, burgers, dips and added to casseroles, lasagna, pizza, salad dressings. It can be scrambled, baked and makes a wonderful sandwich with a jerk or bar be que.

As well as having a high protein content, Tofu also contains calcium, iron, and vitamins B1 and B3. The protein from soy is complete. It has all eight essential amino acids.

BAKED TOFU

1. Cut 1 block tofu into thin slices.

2. Place tofu in bowl.

3. Sprinkle spices evenly over tofu.

4. Add liquid aminos and water. Toss gently.

1   block tofu
1   tsp. basil
1   tsp. paprika
½   tsp. rosemary
2½ tbsp. liquid aminos (for marinade)
¼   cup water (for marinade)
1   tbsp. vegetable oil

To Bake:

1. Spread oil in flat pan, carefully arrange tofu in the pan and bake for 15-20 minutes or until brown at 350 degrees,   Turn after 10 minutes so that both sides can be browned.

Yields: 4 Servings

BLACK SESAME TOFU STIR FRY

1 block tofu (cut into cubes and marinated in nama soya
½ red pepper (diced)
½ yellow/orange pepper (diced)
½ green pepper (diced)
1 cup broccoli flowerets

1 cup mung bean sprouts
¼ cup mushrooms (sliced)
1 tbsp. black sesame seeds
2 cups snow peas
¼ cup nama soya

1. Cook tofu in skillet, or brown lightly in oven at 300°F.

2. Add peppers, mushrooms, sprouts, peas, and all vegetables.

3. Stir occasionally until vegetables are slightly crisp.

4. Garnish with black sesame seeds. Serve hot with ginger sauce.

Yields: 4 servings

SCRAMBLED TOFU

1   16 oz. block of tofu
1   tsp. tamari sauce (to taste)
1½ tbsp. oil

½ tsp. basil
2 tbsp. nutritional yeast
¼ tsp tamari or salt substitute
½ tbsp. garlic powder
1 tsp. vege sal

1. Crumble tofu into a bowl.

2. Melt margarine in skillet, add tofu,
   and dry seasonings. Cook for 2 minutes
   stirring occasionally.

3. Add tamari and salt, cook for 4-5 minutes
   more. Turn heat off. Serve hot.

   Additional spices can be added to
   your taste. Onion powder, parsley flakes, basil.

Yields: 4 servings

TIP: Tofu is available in health food stores and some supermarkets.

NEAT HEBREWS

1 tbsp. olive oil
1 medium onion, diced
8 ounces tempeh, tvp or tofu
   crumbled
2 tbsp. tamari or salt substitute

½ cup ketchup
1 tsp prepared yellow mustard
1 tsp apple cider vinegar
1 tsp sweetener of your choice
4 whole-grain burger buns split

1. Place the oil in a medium saucepan and heat over medium-high.
   When hot, add the onion, tempeh, tvp or tofu, and tamari,
   and sauté them until the onion is tender and lightly browned,
   about 10 minutes.

2. Add the remaining ingredients, except the buns, and mix well.
   Simmer uncovered for 10 minutes, stirring often. Divide the
   hot mixture equally among the buns and serve at once.

Yields: 4 servings

TOFULAFELS

1 cup celery & peppers
   (chopped/sauté)
1 tbsp. garlic powder
1 tbsp. apple cider vinegar
1 tbsp. whole wheat flour
2 tbsp. coriander
½ tsp. sea salt
½ cup onions (chopped fine)

1 lb. tofu
⅓ tsp. sweet basil
3 oz. wheat germ
1 tsp. cumin
1½ tbsp. oil
dry batter mix

1. Mix all ingredients well, except batter. Shape into 1 inch balls.

2. Roll each ball in dry batter.

3. Brown ball in skillet or in 350°F oven with a small amount of oil. If ball crumbles, add water by spoonfuls until they hold.

Yields: 25 Balls

It is written that it is not by bread alone that one can live, but by every word which proceeds from the mouth of the Lord

Main Dishes
Legume

Chickpea Patties

Chickpea Loaf

Handburgers (Lentil Patties)

Simple Middle East Tacos

Stuffed Bell Peppers

Watchi (Ghanian Blackeyed Peas and Rice)

CHICKPEA PATTIES

¼ cup onions diced
½ cup red and green peppers, diced
2 tbsp. cornmeal
¼ cup oil

2 cups chickpeas soaked
½ cup whole wheat flour
2 tbsp. coriander
¼ cup tamari

1. Grind chick peas in blender or food processor with just enough water to make mixture smooth.

2. Place chick peas in mixing bowl and add vegetables and dry ingredients.

3. Stir in tamari, mix well, and then shape into patties.

4. Cook patties on each side in a cast iron skillet with 1 tbsp. of oil or place on oiled baking sheet and back at 300°F until golden brown on both sides.

Yields: 10 Patties

CHICK PEA LOAF

1 lb cooked chick peas
⅓ cup onions (chopped fine)
1 tsp. sea salt
½ tbsp. tamari sauce (optional)
1 tbsp. chick pea flour or whole wheat flour

⅓ cup celery (chopped fine)
⅓ cup oil
2 tbsp. parsley (chopped fine)
1 tsp. dried sage (ground)
1 cup tomato basil sauce

1. In grinder or food processor, add a small amount of water and grind chick peas; add ingredients to chickpeas and mix well.

2. Put in shallow, well oiled baking dish.

3. Bake at 320 degrees for 40 minutes.

4. Spread tomato basil sauce on top and bake 10-12 minutes more.

Yields: 8 servings

HANDBURGERS (LENTIL PATTIES)

½ lb. brown lentils (soaked)
¼ cup onions (chopped fine)
¼ cup red peppers (chopped
    fine)
2 cloves garlic (minced)
⅛ cup tamari sauce

⅛ cup water (to blend)
¼ cup celery (chopped fine)
1 cup oil
1 tsp. paprika
sea salt (to taste)

1. Process soaked lentils in food processor or blender, using fine
   chopper, along with onions, celery, peppers and garlic.

2. Add 1/8 cup water and 1/2 cup oil and spices as you process for a
   smooth but firm mix, skillet, or drop onto baking sheet and brown
   on both sides in 300°F oven.

3. Drop by tablespoon into hot skillet, brown on both sides, using
   2 tsp. oil per skillet.

Yields: 10 Patties

SIMPLE MIDDLE EAST TACOS

1 package tortilla shells
2 cloves garlic (crushed)
¾ tsp. ground coriander
1 cup shredded lettuce
½ cup soy cheese*
½ cups dried kidney beans (soaked
    24 hours)

¼ cup tahini
2 tbsp. lemon juice
½ tsp. cumin
1 cup tomatoes (diced)
1 cup onions (diced)

* follow recipe on page 13

1. Pressure beans in water 3 inches over beans for 45 minutes. Pour off
   water.

2. Puree together beans, tahini, garlic, lemon juice, cumin and coriander.

3. Let stand one-half hour at room temperature. Fill tortilla shells with
   mixture. Place sandwiches in 350°F oven for six minutes. Take out and
   layer garnishes of lettuce, tomato, onions and soy cheese.

Yields: 8-10 servings

STUFFED BELL PEPPERS

½ tbsp. sea salt
1 tsp. maple syrup
1 tbsp. oregano
½ tsp. thyme
2 cups cooked brown rice
12 oz. can tomato paste
9 medium bell peppers
2 tbsp. fresh garlic (crushed)
2 cups soy cheese *

½ lb unseasoned/browned hand
   burger mix
1 medium bell pepper (diced)
½ stick non-hydrogenated
   soy margarine
2½ medium onions (diced)
½ lb. mushrooms (sliced)
1½ tbsp. tamari sauce

* follow recipe on page 13

1. Sauté margarine, onions, peppers and mushrooms. Add garlic powder and tamari sauce. Cover and steam 5 minutes.

2. Mix browned handburger mix, rice and remaining ingredients to steamed vegetables.

3. Slice tops and core bell peppers. Steam for 10 minutes or until slightly tender.

4. Make sauce, mixing tomato paste, maple syrup, oregano, thyme, and fresh garlic. Bring to boil, cover, let stand.

5. Stuff handburger mix into bell peppers, leaving room at the top for ½ tbsp. tomato sauce and ½ tbsp. soy cheese. Bake for 45 minutes at 325 degrees.

Yields: 8 servings

WATCHI (GHANIAN BLACKEYE PEAS AND RICE)

Soak 2 cups of black eye peas overnight
(Note): Beans will swell twice their size.)
⅓ *cup of each vegetable carrots, onions,broccoli, green & red peppers - chopped fine*
4 *cloves garlic*

½ *tbsp. vege sal*
1 *tsp. basil*
1 *tsp. parsley flakes*
1 *tsp. cumin*
1 *tsp. garlic powder*
1 *tsp. onion powder*
2 *tsp. braggs amino*
1 ½ *cupswhole wheat flour*
¼ *cup water*

1. Cook peas with 4 tbsp. oil until almost done.

2 Add salt to taste

3. Add rice to blackeyed peas.

4 Allow to steam

5. Reduce heat, simmer until done.

Sauce

1. Heat 8 oz. oil in skillet.

2. Add flour, stir until brown.

3 Add onions, cook until brown.

4. Add tomato paste and stir until well cooked.

5. Add water according to desired thickness. (It should not be soupy)

6. Add remaining ingredients, allow to cook.

7. Sauce is served over blackeyed peas and rice with salad, greens or any vegetable.

Yields: 26-25 servings

Shopping List

fresh spinach
green beans
lemons
fresh fruit
zucchini
herbal salt
oatmeal
brown rice
parchment paper

Raw Dishes
Salads

Alive Kale Salad

Avocado Salad

Citrus Salad

Cous Cous Salad

Marinated Pickled Beets

Tomato, Cucumber and Sprout Salad

ALIVE KALE SALAD

4 cups kale greens
½ red pepper diced small
½ white onion diced small
3 tbsp. olive oil

¼ tsp sea salt
½ avocado (mashed)
pinch cayenne pepper
squirt of lemon

1. Wash and cut kale greens.

2. Mix in other ingredients.

3. Place salad in serving dish. Add your favorite dressing

Yields:: 3 servings

AVOCADO SALAD

1 medium avocado
2 tbsp. alfalfa sprouts
1 small tomato diced

2 tbsp. olive oil
⅓ onion chopped fine
dash of sea salt

1. Cut avocado in half. Remove seed and spoon avocado out of shell. Chop into medium sized cubes.

2. Add remaining ingredients and mix well.

3. Serve on crackers.

Yields: 2 servings

COUSCOUS SALAD

1 cup couscous soaked
½ red pepper (chopped small)
½ green pepper (chopped small)
½ tsp. sea salt

4 tbsp. olive oil
1 tbsp. spike
3 cloves garlic (chopped fine)
⅓ cup black olives slices
1 tsp. ground cumin

1. Soak couscous in water for 30 minutes. Water should come just above the couscous in a medium size bowl.

2. Allow couscous to absorb all of the water.

3. Separate with a fork.

4. Add all ingredients and mix well.

5. Garnish with parsley.

Yields: 4 servings

CITRUS SALAD

2 oranges
2 grapefruit
¼ cup of raisins (optional)

sprinkling of shredded coconut (optional)
1 kiwi
1 pineapple

Marinated Pickled Beets

⅓ cup apple cider vinegar
½ tsp. olive oil
1 tbsp. chopped tomatoes
vege sal

3 medium beets (shredded)
⅓ cup maple syrup
⅛ tsp. ground cloves
1 tbsp. red onions

1. Mix all ingredients together.

2. Allow to marinate for at least one hour.

Yields: 4 servings

TOMATO, CUCUMBER AND SPROUT SALAD

1 cucumber (chopped fine)
1 tomato (chopped fine)
2 cloves garlic (chopped fine)

¼ cup beans sprouts
¼ cup onions (chopped)
2 tbsp. olive oil
¼ tsp. sea salt (optional)

1. Wash and rinse vegetables. Mix cucumbers, tomato and onions together.

2. Add remaining ingredients. Mix well.

Yields: 2 servings

Raw Dishes

Side Dishes

Almond Salad

Avocado Lettuce Rolls

Avocado Salsa with Olives and Cilantro

Avocado Rice Wraps

Corn Salad

Eggplant Salad

Rainbow Chopped Suey

Raw Sweet Potato

Tofu Salad (Marinated)

Almond Salad

2 cups almond pulp
5 tbsp. soy a naise
2 sticks celery (diced)
2 onions (green onions)

juice from ½ lemon
2-3 tsp. granulated kelp flakes
or powder
3   tbsp. relish

1. Place almond pulp in large bowl.
   (see almond milk recipe).

2. Chop celery and spring onions very
   fine. Add to pulp.

3. Add lemon juice to taste and mix
   in the kelp.

4. Add soy a naise and mix thoroughly.

Yields: 4 servings

*Serving sugestions: Mound the mix on the middle of a plate. Fill half the
plate with mixed leaf salad, and arrange chopped vegetables around sticks of
celery, cucumbers, carrots, or tomatoes or just serve on crackers.*
Serves 4

Avocado Lettuce Rolls

1 bunch romaine lettuce
1 avocado (sliced thin)
1 clove minced garlic
2 scallions chopped fine

1 red pepper (minced)
1 yellow or orange pepper
   minced sunflower sprouts

1. Clean lettuce and separate leaves.

2. Place 2 strips of avocado on a leaf.

3. Top with minced scallions, garlic and a few pieces of peppers and
   some sprouts. Roll carefully tucking in the ends.

4. Secure with a toothpick.

Yields: 2 servings

AVOCADO RICE WRAP

1 *large ripe avocado*
1 *tomato*
½ *cup of peppers red and green*

1 *tbsp. toasted sesame oil*
2 *tbsp. liquid aminos*
1 *package rice wraps*
1 *tbsp. garlic powder*

1. Mix all ingredients together except the rice sheets.

2. Place rice sheet in warm water to soften.

3. Fill with avocado mixture then wrap and serve.

4. Great on a bed of spinach garnished with sunflower sprouts.

You can serve with Ginger Dressing.

Yields: 4 servings

AVOCADO SALSA WITH OLIVES & CILANTRO

1 *small red bell pepper (diced)*
1 *small green bell pepper (diced)*
1 *medium carrot, peeled and sliced*
1 *medium tomato (diced)*
½ *small red onion (diced)*

¾ *cup pitted olives*
¼ *cup fresh lime juice*
½ *tsp. sea salt*
1 *tsp. cayanne pepper*
3 *tbsp. minced cilantro*
2 *ripe avocados (diced small)*

1. Process bell peppers, carrot, tomato and onion to a fine chop in food processor or finely chop by hand.

2. Add remaining ingredients except avocado.

3. Remove ingredients to a bowl and stir in diced avocado.

4. Serve with pita bread or corn chips.

Yields: 4 servings

CORN SALAD

7 large ears of raw corn
¼ cup onion (chopped fine)
½ cup soy butter
1 tbsp. apple cider vinegar

¼ cup red peppers (chopped fine)
¼ cup celery (chopped fine)
1 tbsp. garlic (chopped fine)
1 tsp. liquid aminos, or salt substitute

1. Wash all vegetables.

2. Remove kernels of corn from cob.

3. Mix all ingredients in a large bowl.

4. Serve with your favorite salad.

Yields 4 servings

EGGPLANT SALAD

1 medium eggplant (grated)
3 tbsp. celery (diced fine)
⅓ tsp. sea salt
juice of (1) lemon (optional)
2 cloves fresh garlic
2 cups filtered water
1 tsp cilantro

3 tbsp. onions (diced fine)
2 fresh basil leaves (diced small)
1 small pickle (diced fine)
2 tbsp. red bell pepper (diced fine)
1 tsp. parsley leaves
¼ cup olive oil
½ tsp. garlic powder
3 tbsp. tahini

1. Marinate eggplant for one hour in plain water or lemon water, let stand to drain.

2. Squeeze water out of eggplant.

3. Add diced vegetables and season to taste.

4. Add olive oil, mix well.

5. Place in refrigerator until ready to serve.

6. Top with parsley and serve.

Yields: 3 servings

RAINBOW CHOPPED SUEY

1   cup cauliflower flowerets
1½ cup mung bean sprouts
1   cup broccoli flowerets
1   cup snow peas
2   stalks celery (sliced in long thin strips)
1   carrot (grated on long side)
¼   tsp. sea salt
½   red pepper (sliced thin)
¼   block of firm tofu (cubed)
1   small white or red onion (sliced thin)
7   large mushrooms (thinly sliced)
1   garlic powder
2½ tbsp. liquid aminos, or salt substitute
1 ½ tbsp. toasted sesame oil

1. Marinate vegetables with olive oil and seasonings. Mix well.

2. Add cubed tofu, bean sprouts and toss gently.

3. Serve over Cous Cous, or enjoy as is.

Yields: servings

RAW SWEET POTATO SALAD

3   red sweet potatoes
1½ tbsp. turbinado sugar
¼   tsp. cinnamon
¼ tsp. nutmeg
3 tbsp. soy butter
½ cup raisins
2 tbsp. coconut

1. Grate sweet potatoes on fine side of grater.

2. Add all ingredients and mix well.

3. Chill and serve. Do not refrigerate for more than one day.

Yields: 4 servings

TOFU SALAD (MARINATED)

1 block firm tofu (16 oz)
2 tbsp. tamari sauce, or salt substitute
¼ cup olive oil
½ cup thinly sliced button mushrooms
½ cup thinly sliced onion
½ tsp. garlic powder

1. Cut tofu into cubes.

2. Add sliced onions, mushrooms and all other ingredients.

3. Toss well.

4. Marinate 1-2 hours or to desired taste.

5. Garnish with parsley.

Yields: 4 servings

Tip: The secret of this intensely flavored salad is the long marination; the actual preparation time is only 15 minutes

Easy Sprouting

Sprouts are young shoots that emerge from seeds, beans and grains. During the sprouting process, starch is changed to simple sugar and maintains the B-Complex enabling the sugar to become quick energy.

Sprouting is one of the fastest ways of improving the nutritional value of foods. Almost any whole, natural seed will sprout. Broken seeds or beans will not sprout, neither will heat-treated seeds or beans.

The most popular for sprouting are:
Alfalfa ("King of sprouts")   Lentils
Mung Beans (Oriental cooking)   Wheat Berries

Best length growth:
1- 2 inches   1 ½ - 2 ½ inches
1 inch   1/4 inch

A combination of radish seeds mixed with alfalfa and sprouted together is high in vitamin C and excellent for salads.

DIRECTIONS

Pick over (to get out rocks and broken seeds) and wash 1/4 cup of desired seed or grain; place in quart jar; cover with warm water and soak overnight (cover top of jar with cheese cloth and secure with a rubber-band). Drain off soaking water and rinse with room temperature water and drain again. Keep seeds moist but not wet. Turn jar on its side; keep in warm, dark place until sprouts appear, then place in sunlight. IMPORTANT: Rinse sprouts twice daily for 2 - 5 days, after which time they can be eaten or refrigerated and kept for 3 days at the most.

HAPPY SPROUTING!!!

Salad Dressings, Dips and Relishes

Baht Ami's Dip

Cottage Cheese

Cranberry – Orange Relish

Divine Universal Sisterhood Dressing

Hebrew Dressing

King's Dressing

Lemon & Garlic Dressing

Nicamh's Creamy Butter Dressing

Parsley Dip

Pickles

Sunflower Seed Spread

Sweet Pickle Relish

Thousand Island Dressing

Tofu Garlic Cheese

Tofu Salad Dressing

Tomato Salad Dressing

BAHT AMI'S DIP

1 cup soy butter
2 tbsp. garlic powder
2 tbsp. granulated onion

1 tsp. sea salt
juice of 1 large lemon

1. Make soy butter.

2. Add all dry ingredients and blend well.

3. Blend in lemon juice.

Yields: 1 cup

COTTAGE CHEESE

½ cup crumbled tofu
½ tsp. sea salt

1 tbsp. Baht Ami's Dip
1 tsp. soy butter (see recipe)

1. Place all ingredients in a small bowl.

2. Mix well.

3. Place in mold if desired.

4. Serve with vegetable salad or fruit salad.

Yields: 4 servings

DIVINE UNIVERSAL SISTERHOOD DRESSING

1 medium tomato
½ small onion
3 cloves garlic
1 cup vegetable oil or olive oil

½ cup nutritional yeast
½ cup filtered water
⅛ cup tamari
⅛ cup maple syrup

1. Blend all ingredients in a blender until smooth.

Yields: 2 cups

Note: Nutritional yeast is sometimes used as a dietary supplement to supply vitamin B12

CRANBERRY - ORANGE RELISH

1 lb. fresh cranberries
2 large oranges

1 cup maple syrup
⅛ tsp. ground cloves

1. Wash fruit thoroughly. Squeeze juice from oranges and peel.

2. Grind cranberries and orange peeling separately in blender or food processor.

3. Mix orange juice, maple syrup, ground orange peelings and cranberies in a 2 quart sauce pan. Cook 20 minutes on low heat.

4. Add cloves during the last 10 minutes of cooking time. Serve warm or cold with cornbread dressing

HEBREW DRESSING

1 cup olive oil
1 tsp. paprika
1 small onion

1 tbsp. maple syrup
¼ cup apple cider vinegar
¼ tsp. sea salt

1. Blend all ingredients in a blender until smooth.

Yields: 1 cup

KING'S DRESSING

½ cup red wine vinegar
3 tbsp. herb seasonings
juice of 2 lemons
3 tbsp. garlic powder

1 small onion
tamari sauce (to taste)
3 tbsp. maple syrup

1. Place all ingredients in blender and blend until creamy.

Yields: 1 cup

Lemon Garlic Dressing

juice of 2 lemons
¼ cup tamari sauce
½ cup soy milk
1 tsp. herb dressing

1 cup veg oil
4 garlic cloves

1. Blend milk, lemon, tamari and garlic together in blender.

2. Add oil and seasonings to center until hole closes.

Yields: 3 cups

Nicamah's Creamy Butter Dressing

1 box silken tofu
1 tbsp. apple cider vinegar
½ tsp. sea salt

3 tbsp. nutritional yeast
4 tbsp. soy milk

1. In blender, blend soy milk, nutritional yeast and vinegar.

2. While blending a hole will appear in the middle of the mixture. Slowly pour oil into the middle of the hole until it closes.

Yields:: 2 cups

Parsley Dip

1 cup soy butter
2 cloves garlic

¼ cup fresh parsley
sea salt to taste

1. Add parsley, garlic and salt to soy butter in blender.

2. Blend well until creamy.

Yields: 1 cup

PICKLES

2 lbs. cucumbers
5 pieces pickling spice
5 cloves crushed garlic
3 bay leaves
¼ cup apple cider vinegar
1 tbsp. lemon salt
1 tbsp sea salt
1 gallon boiling hot filtered water
½ cup fresh dill

1. Place all ingredients in a gallon jar.
   Pour boiling hot water over cucumbers.
   Let set for 5-7 days in a dark place.

   Yields: 2 lbs pickles

SUNFLOWER SEED SPREAD

1 cup sunflower seeds
1 tbsp. peppers (chopped fine)
1 tbsp. onions (chopped fine)
1 tbsp. celery (chopped fine)
1 tbsp. pickle relish with juice
1 tsp. fresh lemon juice
2 tsp. liquid aminos
½ tsp. granulated garlic

1. Grind sunflower seeds in blender or food processor.

2. Add all other ingredients to grounded seeds.

3. Mix well. Serve on crackers, toast or as a dip.

   Yields: 4 servings

SWEET PICKLE RELISH

¼ lb. bell peppers (chopped)
¼ lb. turbinado sugar
½ cup apple cider vinegar
juice of 3 lemons

3½ lbs. cucumbers (grated large)
2 lbs. onions (chopped)
1 bulb garlic
4 whole cloves
2 tbsp. vege sal

1. Grate cucumbers and peppers on large side of grater and set aside.

2. Place remaining ingredients in a large pot and bring to a boil.

3. Add cucumbers and peppers. Remove from heat.

4. Omit as much juice as desired. Let cool. Store in a large gallon jar in a cool place for 5-7 days. The longer they sit, the better the flavor.

Yields: 3 ½ lbs.

THOUSAND ISLAND DRESSING

1 small tomato
1 stalk celery
2 tbsp. maple syrup
½ olive oil

½ box silken tofu
½ green pepper
⅓ onion
⅓ cup pickle relish

1. Place onion, celery and tomato into blender.

2. Add silken tofu and remaining ingredients.

3. Blend until creamy.

Yields: 2 cups

TOFU GARLIC CHEESE

1½ lbs. crumbled tofu
1 tbsp. nutritional yeast
1 tsp. sea salt

1 tbsp. soy butter
2 tbsp. crushed garlic

1. In a medium bowl, mix tofu and all other ingredients well.

2. Serve on crackers or toast.

Serves: 2 cups

TOFU SALAD DRESSING

½ block tofu
⅓ cup olive oil
½ tsp. basil
½ tsp. oregano
½ tsp. garlic powder

½ tsp. onion powder
1¼ cup filtered water
1 tbsp. apple cider vinegar
2 tbsp. tamari

1. Puree all ingredients in blender until smooth and creamy.

Serves: 2 cups

HERBAL TOMATO RED PEPPER DRESSING

3 ripe tomatoes
3 cups spring water
2 cloves medium size garlic
1 cup vegetable oil
½ large red peppers (or 1
    whole small red pepper)
¼ medium size yellow onions
¼ cup maple syrup

¼ cup apple cider vinegar
4 tbsp. liquid aminos
2 tbsp. basil
2 tbsp. parsley dried
2 tsp. sea salt
1 tbsp. italian seasonings
1 tbsp. paprika

1. Cut tomatoes in fourths and put in blender.

2. Add remaining ingredients, except oil.

3. Blend all ingredients together for 10 seconds on high.

4. While mixture is blending, slowly pore the oil in the center of the hole that is formed during the blending process.

5. Blend for another 10 seconds.

6. Chill dressing in refrigerator for 20 minutes before serving.

Yields: 8 oz (1 blender full)

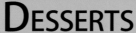

DESSERTS

Almond Surprise Cookies
Apple Nut Cake
Banana Cream Pie
Banana Nut Bread
Basic Living Pie Crust
Birooreet's Carob Peanut Pie
Birooreet's Tropical Pie
Bread Pudding
Carob Chip Pecan Cookies
Carob Cream Pie
Carrot Cake
Coconut Cream Pie
Crunchy Caramel Apples
Dried Fruit Candy
Fruit and Nut Cookies
Fruit Salad
Nutty Mango Delight
Oatmeal Coconut Cookies
Oatmeal Raisin Bars
Pecan Cookies
Pie Crust
Spice Cookies
Strawberry Heaven
Strawberry Jam Pinwheels
Strawberry Shortcake
Strawberry topping

Almond Surprise Cookies

2 cups evaporated cane juice
3 cups unbleached flour
2 sticks non hydrogenated soy margarine

1 tbsp. almond extract
1 cup almond milk
1 cup slivered almonds

1. Mix soy margarine and cane juice to a creamy, fluffy texture.

2. Add flour and milk gradually.

3. Add chopped nuts and remaining ingredients. Stir well.

4. Place by the spoonful on a greased cookie sheet.

5. Bake at 350 degree for 25 minutes.

Yields: 2 dz.

Apple Nut Cake

3 cups whole wheat flour (sifted)
2 tsp. cinnamon
1 tsp. vanilla extract
1 cup apple sauce
2 sticks of non-hydrogenated
    soy margarine

2 cups evaporated cane juice
½ tsp. sea salt
1⅓ cup vanilla soy milk
⅔ cup filtered water
1 cup raisins
1 cup walnuts (chopped)

1. Preheat oven to 350 degrees. Grease and flour a bundt pan.

2. In a large bowl, cream evaporated cane juice and soy margarine together. Stir in remaining ingredients except raisins and nuts.

3. Mix on medium high speed for two (2) minutes. Fold in raisins and nuts.

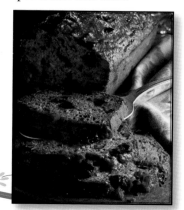

4. Pour into prepared pan. Bake 55 minutes or until toothpick inserted in center comes out clean.

Yields: 8 servings

BANANA CREAM PIE

2 14oz blocks soft tofu
(packed in water)
½ cup vegetable oil
1 cup vanilla soy milk
¾-1 cup maple syrup

1 tsp vanilla extract
2 large mashed bananas
2 tsp agar agar
¼ cup filtered water

1 baked pie crust

1. Place all ingredients except bananas, agar agar and water into a blender.

2. Blend until smooth. Bring water to a boil in a saucepan. Fold in mashed bananas.

3. Stir in agar agar until dissolved and thickened.

4. Pour into blender and thoroughly mix.

5. Pour into a 9 inch baked pie crust. Chill at least four hours before serving.

Yields: 8 servings

BANANA NUT BREAD

2½ cups whole wheat flour
1 cup evaporated cane juice
3½ tsp baking powder
3 tbsp corn oil
2 tbsp egg replacer

4 tbsp water
¾ cup soy milk
3 mashed ripe bananas (1 cup)
1 tsp vanilla
1 cup chopped walnuts

1. Mix liquid ingredients in mixer. Combine dry ingredients.

2. Mix dry ingredients into the wet and fold in bananas Beat at medium speed for 3 minutes.

3. Stir in walnuts at the very end. Grease and flour a 9x5x3 inch pan.

4. Bake in a 350 degree oven for 60 minutes or until done. Cool completely before slicing.

Yields: 8 servings

BASIC LIVING PIE CRUST

3 cups of nuts (almonds, walnuts, ½ pound organic dates
pecans or any combination) 1 tsp. maple syrup (optional)
1 tsp vanilla flavor

1. Place nuts in a food processor and process until nuts are grounded to flour.

2. Add vanilla, than dates and process well.

3. Add maple syrup and process well.

4. Press mixture into a pie pan until entire pie pan is covered.

5. Place the crust in a plastic bag until ready to fill. Crust may be made ahead of time and refrigerated or frozen.

Yield: 1 each 9 inch pie pan

BIROOREET'S CAROB PEANUT BUTTER PIE

1¼ cups almonds 2 cups peanut butter
1 cup chopped dates 1 cup carob powder
2 tsp vanilla 2 tsp. maple syrup or your choice
¼ cup almond milk of sweetener

1. Place almonds in a food processor and grind until powdery.

2. Add dates as it processes until crust holds together.

3. Add 1 tsp vanilla and 1 tsp. maple syrup to the crust.

4. Press the crust into an 8 or 9 in pie pan.

5. In a blender, combine peanut butter, carob powder, vanilla, and maple syrup. Blend until smooth.

6. Add almond milk and blend until creamy.

7. Pour filling into the crust and place the pie in the refrigerator to chill.

Yields: 8 servings

BIROOREET'S TROPICAL DREAM PIE

1¼ cup almonds
1   cup chopped dates
½   cup macadamia nuts
3   tsp vanilla
1   cup blueberries
4   bananas

3   mangos
½   cup strawberries
¼   cup coconut milk
½   cup shredded coconut
3   kiwi
3   tsp. maple syrup

1. Process almonds until powdery and begin to add dates to the processor until the crust holds together.

2. Add 1 tsp. each vanilla flavor and maple syrup to taste.

3. Press the crust into a 8 to 9 inch pie pan.

4. Process macadamia nuts and put to the side.

5. Wash, peel and slice all fruit thinly except for the blueberries.

6. Blend blueberries and add maple syrup, vanilla, 1 banana, 1 mango, and coconut milk to the blueberry mix and blend until smooth.

7. Fold in chopped fruit (mangos, strawberries, and kiwi, save some kiwi for garnish).

8. Place a layer of sliced bananas on the pie crust.

9. Pour the blueberry pie filling into the crust.

10. Sprinkle macadamia nuts on top and garnish with sliced kiwi and shredded coconut.

Yields: 8 servings

BREAD PUDDING

2½ cups warm soy milk
1 tsp vanilla extract
1 tbsp egg replacer
1 cup raisins
1 cup chopped pecans

2 sticks non hydrogenated soy margarine
½ cup evaporated cane juice
5 cups whole wheat bread (cubed)
1 tsp cinnamon
¾ tsp nutmeg

1. Cream margarine and sugar.

2. Add all other ingredients. Mix well.

3. Place in an 8x8 in square pan.

4. Bake for one (1) hour at 345 degrees.

Yield: 8 servings

CAROB CHIP COOKIES

¼ cup vitasoy vanilla milk
1 tsp vanilla extract
½ cup carob chips
Nut pieces (almonds, walnuts, or pecans)

2½ cups pastry flour
1½ sticks no salt non-hydrogenated soy margarine
1¼ cups turbinado sugar

1. Cream margarine and sugar together.

2. Add vanilla and milk.

3. Add carob chips. Mix in flour. (Optional- add coconuts and raisins or nuts.)

4. Add more flour if dough is sticky.

5. Place mixture on a greased sheet pan in small balls.

6. Press balls flat and bake 10 –12 minutes.

7. Remove from sheet pan and place cookies on a cooling rack.

Yields: 25 cookies.

Carob Chip Macadamia Nut Cookies

2 sticks non hydrogenated
soy margarine
2 cups cane sugar
3 cups flour (unbleached)
1 cup vanilla soy milk

1 tsp vanilla extract
1 cup carob chips
1 cup macadamia nuts

1. Cream sugar and margarine until fluffy.

2. Add flour, milk and vanilla.

3. Mix ingredients thoroughly.

4. Stir in chips and chopped nuts.

5. Use cookie scoops and place on sheet.

6. Bake @ 345 degrees for 8 minutes.

Yields: 2 dz

Carob Chip Pecan Cookies

1½ cups evaporated cane sugar
2 sticks non-hydrogenated
soy margarine
3 cups whole wheat flour (sifted)

1 cup soy milk
1 cup non dairy carob chips
1 cup pecan nuts
1 tsp. vanilla extract

1. Cream margarine, sugar and vanilla together.

2. Gradually add flour and soy milk.

3. Fold in carob chip and pecans.

4. Mix well.   Spoon onto greased
   baking sheets.

5. Bake at 350 degrees for 12 minutes.
   Place cookies on baking racks to cool.

Yields: 3 dz.

CAROB CREAM PIE

1   tsp. vanilla extract
¼   cup carob powder
2   tsp. agar agar
¼   cup filtered water
1   baked pie crust

2 -14 oz. blocks soft tofu (packed in water)
½   cup vegetable oil
1   cup vanilla soy milk
¾-1 cup maple syrup

1. Place all ingredients except carob powder, agar agar and water into a blender.

2. Blend until smooth. Bring water to a boil in a saucepan. Fold in carob powder.

3. Stir in agar agar until dissolved and thickened.

4. Pour into blender and thoroughly mix.

5. Pour into a 9 inch baked pie crust. Chill at least four hours before serving.

Yields: 8 servings

CARROT CAKE

2 cups turbinado raw sugar
3 cups carrot pulp
1 cup carrot juice
3 cups whole wheat flour
2 sticks non-hydrogenated
  soy margarine

1 tsp cinnamon
1 tsp nutmeg
1 cup raisins
1 cup chopped walnuts

1. Cream margarine and sugar in a mixer.

2. Add all other ingredients and mix well.
   Stir in raisins and walnuts. Grease and flour a 9x12 in pan.

3. Spread mix in the prepared pan.

4. Bake in a 325 degree oven for 1 hour and 10 minutes or until
   firm in the middle.

Yields: 8 servings

COCONUT CREAM PIE

2   14 oz. blocks soft tofu
    (packed in water)
½   cup vegetable oil
1   cup vanilla soy milk
¾-1 cup maple syrup

1 tsp. coconut extract
½ cup shredded coconut
2 tsp. agar agar
¼ cup filtered water
1 baked pie crust

1. Place all ingredients except shredded coconut, agar agar and
   water into a blender.

2. Fold in shredded coconut.

3. Bring water to a boil in a saucepan and stir in agar agar until dissolved
   and thickened.

4. Pour into blender and thoroughly mix.

5. Pour into a 9 inch baked pie crust. Chill at least four hours
   before serving.

Yields: 8 servings

CRUNCHY CARAMEL APPLES

3 *large red delicious apples*
   (pared and sliced into rings)
3 *tbsp. non-hydrogenated soy margarine*
2 *tbsp. cold pressed olive oil*
¾ *cup evaporated cane juic*

1 *tsp. blackstrap molasses*
¼ *cup filtered water*
1 *tsp. cinnamon*
½ *cup chopped walnuts*
¼ *cup raisins*

1. Sauté walnuts in olive oil and margarine in large skillet until lightly toasted.   Remove from pan.

2. Brown apple rings on both sides until just tender. Place apples and walnuts in a shallow dish.

3. Combine cane juice, water, and molasses in skillet. Stir and heat until sugar dissolves.

4. Bring to a boil.   Pour over apple mixture. Serve warm.

Yields: 3 servings

DRIED FRUIT CANDY

½ *lb organic raisins*
½ *lb organic figs*
¼ *lb coconut*

½ *lb organic dates*
¼ *lb walnuts (crushed)*

1. Cut fruit into small pieces and mix well.

2. Add crushed nuts a little at a time.

3. Shape into balls and roll each ball into the coconut.

Variations: Use any dried fruits such as prunes, apricots, etc.
* Does not have to be refrigerated.

Yields: 2 dz.

FRUIT AND NUT COOKIES

2 sticks non-hydrogenated soy margarine
2 cups evaporated cane juice
3 cups sifted whole wheat flour
1 tsp vanilla extract

1 cup vanilla soy milk
1 cup chopped dates
1 cup chopped walnuts

1. Cream margarine and sugar.

2. Add flour, vanilla extract, and soy milk.

3. Mix until smooth.

4. Stir in dates and walnuts. Spoon on greased baking sheet.

5. Bake in a 350 degree oven 10-12 minutes or until golden brown.

FRUIT SALAD

7 peaches
5 mangoes
3 bananas
2 apples

2 pints strawberries
¼ cup raisins
2 tbsp. wheatgerm
2 tbsp. maple syrup or agave nectar

1. Blend ½ pint of strawberries, 2 peaches, and 1 banana with sweetener of your choice to make the sauce.

2. Chop remaining fruit; place in mixing bowl and add raisons. Mix well.

3. Top with sauce and wheatgerm.

4. Serve chilled.

NUTTY MANGO DELIGHT

1 mango (diced)
¼ cup raisins

½ cup chopped nuts (your choice)
8 oz. soy ice cream.

1. Place one scoop of soy ice cream in a small dish.

2. Top with fruit and nuts.

Yields: 1 servings

Oatmeal Coconut Cookies

1 stick non-hydrogenated soy margarine
1 tsp. vanilla extract
1 cup oatmeal
⅔ cup soy milk

1 cup pastry flour (sifted)
1 cup coconut
¼ cup walnuts
1 tsp. cinnamon
1 cup turbinado raw sugar

1. Cream margarine, sugar and vanilla extract together in mixing bowl.

2. Mix oatmeal and coconut together. Add this dry mix to the margarine mixture gradually alternating with the soy milk.

3. Blend in the flour gradually. Mix well.

4. Spoon onto greased oven pan. Flatten with a fork and bake at 350 degrees for eight (8) minutes.

Yields: 1½ dz.

Oatmeal Raisin Bars

1 tbsp. maple syrup
½ cup dates
½ cup raisins

1 cup walnuts
1 cup oats
2 tbsp. blackstrap molasses

1. Chop walnuts and dates into small pieces

2. Mix all ingredients well.

3. Place mix into a 9 x 9 square pan.

4. Refrigerate for one (1) hour.

5. Cut into square bars.

Yields: 4 servings

PECAN COOKIES

2 sticks non-hydrogenated
soy margarine
2 cups evaporated cane juice
3 cups whole wheat flour

1 tsp vanilla extract
1 cup vanilla soy milk
1 cup chopped pecans

1. Cream cane juice and margarine. Add flour, vanilla and soy milk.

2. Mix until smooth. Stir in pecans and shape into small cookies.

3. Bake in 350 degree oven for 10-12 minutes or until golden brown

Yields: 2 dz.

PIE CRUST

2 cups whole wheat flour
¼ tsp. sea salt

4 tbsp. non-hydrogenated soy margarine
4-6 tbsp. ice cold water

1. Mix flour and salt in bowl.

2. Slice margarine into flour. Using a pastry blender, incorporate margarine into flour until mixture is crumbly.

3. Add water one tablespoon at a time. Mix until flour just binds. Divide in half.

4. Roll half to cover bottom of a 9 inch pie plate. Bake according to pie directions.

5. Fill with your favorite fruit filling. Roll remaining dough and cover pie.

SPICE COOKIES

3 cups whole wheat flour
2 tsp. vanilla extract
1 tsp. nutmeg
2 cups evaporated cane juice

1 tbsp. blackstrap molasses
1 tsp. cinnamon
2 sticks non-hydrogenated soy margarine
1 cup vanilla soy milk

1. Cream soy margarine and sugar. Add molasses and vanilla.

2. Mix until blended. Add all other ingredients.
   Mix until just blended.

3. Drop by heaping teaspoons.
   Flatten with a fork.

4. Bake in a 350 degree oven for 17
   minutes or until brown on the bottom.

Yields: 2 dozen.

STRAWBERRY HEAVEN

1 block silken tofu
4 medium bananas
½ lb. strawberries
3 tbsp. agave nectar
2 tbsp. coconut extract

2 tbsp. toasted wheatgerm
2 tbsp. chopped nuts
¼ tsp. cinnamon
3 tbsp. soy milk

1. Blend tofu with soy milk and agave sweetener.

2. Slice bananas and strawberries.

3. In a small dessert dish, layer banana, cream mixture and strawberries
   until all ingredients are used.

4. Add a last layer of cream and top with a mixture of toasted wheatgerm,
   coconut and nuts.

• This is a wonderful fruit recipe and can be created with any combination of non-citrus fruit that is in season, such as mangoes or peaches.

• Can be eaten as a breakfast or dessert.

Yield: 4 servings

STRAWBERRY JAM

1 pint strawberries (crushed)
4 cups raw sugar
⅜ cup prepared natural fruit pectin (using 4 oz box)

1. Wash, stem and crush strawberries with a potato masher.

2. Add sugar. Let sit for 10 minutes.

3. Stir occasionally. Prepare powdered fruit pectin according to directions. It should make ¾ cup hot mixture.

4. Add 3/8 cup to the strawberries.

5. Stir for 3 minutes until sugar dissolves completely.

6. Store in plastic container with tight fitting lid.

7. Freeze until set. Thaw in refrigerator.

Note: Will keep in refrigerator for three weeks.

STRAWBERRY JAM PINWHEELS

2 sticks non- hydrogenated soy margarine
2 cups evaporated cane juice
3 cups unbleached all purpose flour
1 cup vanilla soy milk
1 tsp vanilla extract

1. Cream margarine and sugar until light and fluffy.

2. Add remaining ingredients and mix on medium speed until smooth. (approx. 1 minute)

3. On a floured surface, roll dough ⅛ inch thick.

4. Cut into 4 inch squares. Cut each corner in half not cutting through the middle. Place small amount of strawberry jam in middle of square.

5. Fold alternating corner toward the center making the shape of a pinwheel.

6. Bake in a 350 degree oven for 10 -12 minutes or until golden brown.

Yields: 24-30 pinwheels

STRAWBERRY SHORTCAKE

½ cup evaporated cane juice
2 cups whole wheat flour
1 tbsp. non aluminum baking powder
½ cup non-hydrogenated soy margarine

¾ cup soy milk
1 tbsp. egg replacer
4 tbsp. filtered water

1. Cream evaporated cane juice and non-hydrogenated soy margarine together.

2. Add all other ingredients and mix well.

3. Spread mixture in a prepared 9 inch round pan bake in a 375 degree oven for 25-30 minutes. Cool completely.

4. Split the shortcake in two layers. Serve topped with sliced strawberries and vegan whipped topping.

Yields: 8 servings

STRAWBERRY TOPPING

1 pint strawberries sliced
¾ cup evaporated cane juice

1. Mix strawberries and sweetener in a bowl.

2. Let sit for 10 minutes.

Serve on ice cream or cake.

Yields: 1 pint

"And the Lord God planted a garden eastward in Eden; and there he put the man whom he had formed."

And out of the ground made the Lord God to grow every tree that is pleasant to the sight, and good for food; the tree of life also in the midst of the garden, and the tree of knowledge of good and evil."

Genesis 2: 8-9

DRINKS

Banana Boom

Carrot Drink

Ginger Get Well

Green Power

Hot Carob Drink

Island Paradise

Kiwi Sip

Lemon Mist

Mellow Mellon Shake

Peanut Maple Drink

Sesame Milk

Seventh Heaven Vegetable
Juice

Soy Milk

Very Berry Fine

Banana Boom

2 frozen banana (peel before
    freezing)
1 cup almond milk
1 tbsp. raw tahini

1 tbsp. wheat germ
2 tbsp. maple syrup
1 tsp. blackstrap molasses

1. Mix all ingredients in a blender.

Carrot Drink

2 lbs carrots equal to 2 cups
    after juicing
1 tsp. nutmeg
½ cup grated coconut

¼ cup maple syrup
1 cup soy milk
2 cups filtered water

1. Pre – wash and scrape carrots until clean.

2. Juice carrots. Carrot juice can be strained if desired.

3. Add remaining ingredients to carrot juice and blend. Can be
served with ice.

Yields: 16 oz.

Ginger Get Well

2 pieces fresh gingerroot
1 cup pineapple cubes
1 orange (juiced)

½ cup ice
⅓ cup pure maple syrup
1 tsp. ground nutmeg

1. Juice or mince the ginger. Each piece about 6 inches long; peeling
is optional.

2. Combine all the ingredients in a blender and process
until smooth.

Yields: 16 ozs.   This recipe is contributed by: "Juice Power"

GREEN POWER

1 cup spinach
1 cucumber
3 stalks celery
½ cup parsley

2 tomatoes
1 small red pepper
1 clove garlic

1. Blend all ingredients in a blender until smooth.

Yields: 2 cups

HOT CAROB DRINK

½ cup carob powder
3 cups soy milk
2 tsp. agave nectar
1 tbsp vanilla

Yields: 4 servings

1. Place all ingredients in a blender and blend.

2. Heat and serve or drink cold.

ISLAND PARADISE

1 cup fresh papaya
8 oz. pineapple juice
4 oz. coconut milk
1 tsp. maple syrup

Yields: 2 cups

1. Blend until smooth.

KIWI SIP

4 kiwifruit
½ cup ice cubes
⅔ cup almond milk
1 tbsp. maple syrup

Yields: 3 servings

1. Peel and chop kiwi fruit.

2. Combine all ingredients in a blender and process until smooth.

LEMON FLUSH

2 tbsp. lemon juice
8 oz. filtered water
1 tbsp. maple syrup

Yields: 1 cup

1. Mix all ingredients together.

LEMON MIST

1½ cups filtered water
juice of 4 medium lemons
½ cup maple syrup
10 ice cubes(about 1 ½ cups)

Yields: 2 – 16 oz servings

1. Blend water, lemon juice and maple syrup.

2. Add ice cubes and blend.

MELLOW MELLON SHAKE

½ canolope
½ cup filtered water

1. Cut canolope in half, scoop out seeds and peel.
2. Blend all ingredients. Add sweetener if desired.

PEANUT MAPLE DRINK

⅓ cup creamy peanut butter
⅛ tsp. vanilla flavor
3 tbsp. maple syrup

8 oz. filtered water
1 cup ice

1. Blend all ingredients in blender on medium speed.

Yields: 2 servings

ALMOND MILK

1 cup almond nuts (soak 8 hours)
2½ cup filtered water

1. Rinse soaked almond nuts.

2. In a blender, combine the almonds with filtered water.

3. Blend thoroughly and strain twice with a cheese cloth.

4. Add a few dates, maple syrup, or your favorite sweetener.   This milk will keep 2 – 3 days.

Yields: 2 cups

SEVENTH HEAVEN/ VEGETABLE JUICE

2 lbs. carrots
½ cucumber
½ celery stalk
1 small beet

½ small tomato
4 oz fresh parsley
½ small red bell pepper

1. Wash all vegetables well and juice in an electric juicer.

2. Strain in a cheese cloth or drink as is.

Yields 2 servings

SOY MILK

½ cup soy flour (sifted)
3 cups filtered water

1. Combine flour and 2 cups water in bowl to form a paste.

2. Place remaining water in small pot. Add paste. Stir constantly over low heat. Allow mixture to come to a boil.

3. Cook until skim appears on top. Remove skim and strain milk.

4. Cool before serving.

VERY BERRY FINE

1 cup papaya juice
¼ cup pure maple syrup
¼ cup blueberries

¼ cup sliced strawberries
    (about 4)
¼ cup ice
1 tbsp. cranberries

1. Combine all the ingredients in a blender and process until smooth.

2. Serve at once or chill briefly in the refrigerator.

Yields: 16 oz.

This recipe is contributed by: "Juice Power

Important Food Supplements Needed For A Balanced Diet

Brewers Yeast
Is rich in minerals, particularly chromium. Chromium helps to lower cholesterol and helps the body maintain normal blood sugar levels and so may help
individuals with diabetes. Contains the complete vitamin B complex
Dosage: 5-7 months: ½ tsp with Breakfast and Dinner
        7 months-3 years: 1 ½ tsp with Breakfast and Dinner
        3-12 Years: 1 tbsp with Dinner
        12 Years-Adult: 1 Heaping tbsp with Dinner

Sesame Seeds (Ground)
An excellent source of calcium, magnesium, iron, copper, zinc, fiber, vitamin
B1, and phosphates. Sesame seeds are the most calcium rich food on the planet.
They also prevent high blood pressure and lower cholesterol. ¼ cup contains
74% RDA for copper and 35.1% RDA for calcium
Dosage: Babies and Children: 3-4 tsp Daily
        Teens and Adults: ½ cup Daily
        Expecting Mothers: 1 cup Daily

Black strap Molasses
An excellent source of iron and calcium. Crude blackstrap molasses has been
used to treat arthritis.
Dosage: 5 months to 3 years: 1 tsp 3 times a day with water Daily
        3 years- Adult: 1 tbsp with 1/3 cup water Daily

Soy Milk/Almond milk/coconut milk
Both soy milk and almond milk are an excellent source of calcium and protein.
Soy beans contain isoflavones which reduce the rate of breast cancer by 50%.
Almonds are the less acidic of all nuts and are also high in magnesium, and
phosphorous. Almonds also act as an anti cancer agent. Coconut milk is very
rich in minerals, particularly high in iron and calcium. Non processed coconut
milk is one of nature's most perfect foods. Coconut milk is a blend of coconut
water and coconut pulp. Coconut water kills intestinal worms, is an excellent diuretic, and contains all of the same electrolytes that are found in human
blood. The coconut water in one average green organic coconut contains 44%
RDA of calcium, 106% RDA of iron.
Dosage: Babies and Children 2 times Daily
        Teens and Adults: 1- 8 oz glass Daily

Fenugreek

Rich in vitamins and minerals and is particularly high in protein. Reduces mucous in sinuses along with asthmatic conditions. Lowers cholesterol. Also increases milk production in nursing mothers. Can be used to treat gout, anemia, and diabetes. Also, aids in digestion and reduces inflammation in boils, wounds, sores, and tumors. Can be taken to help bronchitis and gargled to ease sore throats.

Dosage: 1 tbsp per day

Flax Seeds

Are good for brittle hair. Can be used for all pulmonary infections, especially bronchitis. Also, flax seed delivers the full benefits of Omega 3, 6, & 9 EFAs plus all of the fiber, protein, lignans (anticancer agents), vitamins, minerals, and amino acids that are important for overall good health. Contains 98% more lignans and 97% more fiber than flax seed oil.

Dosage: 1 tbsp per day

Flax seed oil

Is rich in Omega 3 fatty acids (which prevent blood clots in arteries). Strengthens the cardiovascular system, immune system, circulatory system, reproductive system, and nervous system, as well as joints. Can also prevent both colon cancer and breast cancer. Can heal the inner lining of inflamed intestines. Lowers cholesterol, increases energy, increases metabolism, aids in weight loss, and improves absorption of calcium. Can also improve eyesight and relieve some cases of asthma. Treats eczema, psoriasis, and dandruff.

Dosage: 1 tbsp per day

Parsley

Is an effective diuretic and breath freshener. Is good for indigestion, measles, lungs, and spleen. Improves functioning of the kidneys, bladder, prostrate, adrenal gland, and thyroid gland. Is also rich in vitamin A, vitamin C and also is particularly high in iron.

Dosage: Babies and Children: 2 Sprigs Daily
          Teens and Adults: 3 springs Daily

Wheatgerm
High in vitamin A,C, E, selenium, and iron. Wheatgerm should be vacuum packed and refrigerated. Check the label to ensure that it is fresh.
Dosage: 5 months- 6 years: 2 tsp Daily
         6 Years- Adult: 3 tsp Daily

Sprouts
Very rich in vitamin A, B complex , C, D, and E, iron, enzymes, potassium, and magnesium, calcium, phosphorus, amino acids, fatty acids, zinc, and chromium.
Put them in your diet as often as possible

Chick Peas And Soy Beans
Among the highest forms of protein available
Dosage: One serving 2 times a week.
(Serve with brown rice to make a complete protein meal.)

Kelp
High in vitamins and minerals, particularly calcium. Good for goiter and thyroid conditions, good for arthritis, relieves water retention, prevents obesity, protects against heart disease and radiation, removes toxic metals from the body (i.e. fights against environmental pollutants that attack the body). Try it as a salt substitute!
Dosage: 5 months-1 year: ½ tsp Daily
         1-6 Years: 1 tsp Daily
         6 Years to Adult : Tbsp Daily

*Consistency is the key for supplements to be effective.

Restaurant Locations

UNITED STATES

Soul Vegetarian Restaurant
1205 South Adams Street
Tallahassee, FL 32301
(850) 893-8208
www.soulvegtallahassee.com

Everlasting Life Health Complex
9185 Central Avenue
Capital Heights, MD 20743
(301) 324-6900

Soul Vegetarian Exodus
2606 Georgia Ave. NW
Washington, D.C. 20001
(202) EAT-SOUL (328-7685)

Soul Vegetarian East
205 E. 75th St.
Chicago, IL 60619
(773) 224-0104

Soul Vegetarian Restaurant
879 –A. Ralph D. Abernathy Blvd. SW
Atlanta, GA 30310
(404) 752-5194

Soul Vegetarian International
652 North Highland
Atlanta, GA 30306
(404) 874-0145

ISRAEL

Taim Hakaim (A Taste of Life)
43 Ben Yehuda St.
Tel Aviv, Israel
011-972-3-620-3151

GHANA, WEST AFRICA

Assase Pa (The Earth is Good)
AMA Compound-High Street
Accra, Ghana, West Africa
021-0761936

Assase Pa Health & Wellness Resort
Cape Coast, Ghana, West Africa
042-309132

Yafah B. Israel is a dynamic, international leader in nutrition and driving force in the Soul Vegetarian life support family. With over 25 years of experience as a nutritionist, vegan chef, holistic health practitioner, and restaurant dietary consultant, Yafah has shared her talents and insight through radio and television interviews, community nutrition programs, health seminars, vegan cooking demonstrations and workshops around the globe. Among those who have experienced her practical and inspiring message have been major organizations including Morehouse College, the National Council of Negro Women, UNICEF, Lucent Technology/ AT&T, Macy's, Atlanta Chamber of Commerce, and Whole Life Expo. She has been featured in the traveling African American Women on Tour speakers' series. And her recipes have been published in several magazines such as Essence, Vegetarian Times, Upscale, and Heart and Soul. She has made appearances on networks such as CNN and Paramount Studios.

Yafah serves as an Elevated Crown Sister, the highest leadership position for women among the African Hebrew Israelites of Jerusalem. They are committed to presenting a new image of divine womanhood to the world in the home, in business and in politics. In over 35 years, this vegan community based in Israel, has virtually eradicated high blood pressure, cancer, heart disease, the major killers of the modern diet and lifestyle. Researchers from Waverly Bellmont Medical Center, Meharry Medical College and Vanderbilt University found that this community beat the risk of high blood pressure and obesity by making favorable life changes – disproving the notion that African Americans are genetically predisposed to cardio-vascular illness.

Yafah's international travels have provided a platform to exhibit her culinary versatility in creating in dishes desirable to the cultures of the world. They all carry the Soul Vegetarian characteristics of being great-tasting and good for you. Sampling her creative experience in these recipes, it is not hard to understand why Soul Vegetarian remains the largest and most popular vegan-food restaurant chain in the world and a home for all those – vegan, vegetarian or not -- who love good food and living a healthy, vibrant life.

Soul Vegetarian
Cookbook Vol. 2

$19.95 ## Order Form

Name _____

Address _____

_____

City _____ **State** _____ **Zip** _____

Phone _____ **E-mail** _____

I would like to order _____Copies
of Soul Vegetarian Cookbook Vol. 2 at a cost of $19.95 each
+ shipping and handling of $4.00 each.

Total Cost _____

Payment Type Check/Money Order☐ Visa☐ MC☐ AMEX☐

Number _____ **Exp.** _____

Please make checks payable to: **Soul Vegetarian Restaurant**

Mail to: Soul Vegetarian Restaurant 879 Ralph D. Abernathy
Blvd., Atlanta, GA, 30310 (404) 752-5194

For additional information contact:
Publishing Associates, Inc.
5020 Montcalm Drive
Atlanta, GA 30310
fcpublish@aol.com